Introduction

Backed up by soaring music, I will stride into the room and be met with outstretched hands and applause. I will take center stage. I will own the room. I will close this deal.

I'm Jay Kriner, Serial Entrepreneur, Shark Tank Survivor, VIRAL Product Innovator and Business Consultant.

Welcome to the thrilling, twisted, carnival of sales – where each sensation we create is a vibrant performer that takes center stage, where each suggestion we make surges through the crowd with electric hues of emotion. Standing in this crazy circus tent that is life, you, too, will captivate your audience. You too will own the spotlight. Exhilarated, your audience will stand and cheer. And in that moment, you will be able to sell anything.

Your success didn't just happen – you created it. You learned psychology and stage presence and timing and presentation. You learned how to read the room. You learned when to push .... and when to back away. Sales might be natural to some, but it can be mastered by all.

Believe it or not, one of the keys to a great life is being a good salesperson. I'm going to cut right to the chase: every product, every job, and even every relationship is the result of a sale. Think about it: Going to an interview ... sell yourself! Sitting down on a first date ... sell yourself! Needing to move an entire cargo container of doo- hickies ... get busy and sell! If you master the art of selling, you *will* succeed at whatever you put your mind to. This kind of success makes a person happy. And that is the goal.

Beyond success and happiness, those things that make a good salesperson – like understanding psychology and knowing how to communicate effectively – will make your life easier and more complete.

How? Well, it's a matter of understanding people at a deeper level. Ever wonder how you can tell when someone is lying, or when someone is interested in you? Or, how you know that someone is *not* interested in a conversation?

Secret here: Those aren't your Spidey senses at work – but you're not far off. You're actually translating body language – a look, a gesture, even a tone of voice. Understanding body language is a quick way to peek behind a person's mental curtain.

Understanding people is essential to Sales. The better you are at understanding people, the better a salesperson you will be. And, really, the better at life you'll be.

Welcome to my world of never-ending sales and the butterflies you get from the chase. Once you understand how to read people, selling becomes easier. This is because you also will have learned how to more effectively communicate your message to that person. Once you've begun to understand people, your marketing will move people more effectively; your advertising will resonate more powerfully; your PR will engage the right audience.

Reading people, hearing nuance, understanding reactions, even using psychology – all of these go into making a great salesperson. This short book will not only teach you how to use marketing and communication to sell *effectively,* but it will also show you how to apply 'selling' to almost every real-world situation, professional and personal.

In these chapters, there *is* a method to my madness. But you should feel free to just bounce around, too. Each chapter teaches you the what's, whys, and WTFs of sales.

So, sit back, crack open some box wine, and learn ... how to sell anything.

Chapter 1: Perception & Sensory

Ladies and gentlemen, step right up! Welcome to the grand spectacle of perception, where reality wears a cloak of illusion and our minds dance with the tricks of the trade. In this chapter, we will dive headfirst into the captivating world of how to create, and shift, perceptions.

Warning: Perception can set scale, but it can also be misleading. Perception can influence buying choices and can even invoke emotion. It can create desire that overwhelms all else.

Trust me, I know!

In 2017, I made the brilliant decision to attend the FYRE Festival! You know, that crazy, failed, luxury music festival in the Bahamas, that made world headlines, but never happened and that guy who put it together went to prison?!

You heard me right! I bought into all the hype – the perception that FYRE was going to be the 21st century equivalent of Woodstock – but on a glorious Caribbean beach. Famous! History–making! There, I was going to be surrounded by models dancing on beaches and sitting in front of stages where all the top artists were going to perform. It was to be an unstoppable experience. Legendary. Epic.

I had to go. Now, by no means am I one to just book extreme trips, but this was going to be off the charts. So, in just a few clicks, everything was booked and there I was on the first flight out of Miami, headed to Great Exuma in the Bahamas, along with a plane full of other attendees on our way to what was marketed as the most luxurious island music festival EVER!

Buyer beware! Read the fine details and separate facts from frenzied fiction. FYRE tuned out to be a flop – a big one. And I fell for it! Hard.

It wasn't only that it was a flop: it was that the entire marketing scheme made me create bizarre fantasies in my head. Of course, I am known to be the guy who jumps into crazy, hyped-up situations more suited for celebrities than a hardworking, regular guy from Texas. But FYRE sold me. Big time. And I bought into it all. Even the flip-flops.

In retrospect, if you strip away all of the illegalities, what FYRE did was create a phenomenally successful, altered reality or fantasy for a whole bunch of people. The organizers manipulated our perceptions of who we were. What they did was master the manipulation of perception and directly target an audience through a marketing platform focused on reactions to our senses. With just a few short videos and posts, they put us on the beach where we could feel the warm air and white sand, where we could hear the laughter and the pounding music. They imprinted these possibilities on our minds. Sleep was optional.

Perception is the key to advertising. Your message is the product. It should be designed, with words or visuals, to appeal to your target consumer. What you are trying to do is to evoke an emotion by affecting one of the senses. In the case of the FYRE Festival, they appealed to touch, sound, smell, taste, *everything!* All of us who spent hundreds – if not thousands – of dollars for tickets shared the desire for adventure, luxury, music, an exotic locale. *That* is what we were sold.

But it's not just luxury adventures and Caribbean beaches that create desire. A good salesman will often target as many of the 5 senses they can, to create some type of appeal.

The Power of Perception

Picture this: you're strolling through a busy mall on a Saturday morning. You step into your favorite clothing store and the air is filled with this sweet yet musky aroma. Your nose twitches like a Columbian drug dog, and suddenly, you're not just looking for new socks; you must have that captivating scent. Are they selling cologne? They are. You're in!

But hold onto your wallet's folks, because that aromatic journey is no happy accident.

Many destinations, be it your favorite store or a luxurious hotel lobby, strategically use scents to entice or create a lasting impression. Or to sell things. Often, such scents will lead to our impulse buys. Damn those places.

Let's make some sense of those scents.

Your sense of smell is one of the most powerful of
the senses. Smell – whether sweet or musky or "Oh hell no!"
– can influence almost any decision you make. In fact,
scents are widely used to influence not just a meal, but vacation memories and shopping decisions.

I mean, I never *need* a slice of fresh pizza, but just the
smell alone will make me reach for my wallet.

So, knowing that smell has such a heavy impact on
our desires and memories, take a moment to think about
your favorite restaurant or hotel or mall. I bet you can remember a scent that affected your experience at that place.
Oftentimes, the wafting of that scintillating scent was no accident: it was done purposefully to make you remember that
place every time you smelled that scent. After I learned that
venues often deliberately use scent, I had to try it myself!

Not too long ago, my wife and I pulled the trigger
and bought a cabin in north Georgia, to be a rental. Getting
it ready for our first renter, we went to a boutique store and
picked out exactly the scent we wanted to match the feel of
the cabin. We wanted the entire place to have a rich leather
and sweet tobacco scent, so that guests would associate that
cozy smell with their stay. Moreover, if they were to smell it
again, elsewhere, they would remember the cabin and want
to return.

And if a scent wasn't enough, my A.D.D. led to our strategically focusing on our guests' senses when decorating the cabin, from choosing the soft vintage leather couch and the high-end linens, to our deciding to put a putting green on the deck. When it came time to market the rental, I wanted to give a specific perception of cozy, trendy, and luxury through the images we chose. The place quickly booked out with Five Stars and shortly after our first season we received an offer from one of our guests. The cabin was great, but our attention to detail – particularly paying attention to how the cabin appealed to our guests' senses – sealed the deal.

Our brains use our senses like detectives; they're forever on the lookout for clues to unlock hidden memories and emotions. So, when you catch a whiff of that familiar store, your brain plays a game of connect-the-dots, linking the scent to cozy mornings, friendly conversations, and the comforting warmth of your favorite mug.

What is the role of all of these sensory receptors? They hold a key to the gates of our memories.

How much of an impact does, say, our sense of smell play in everyday life? Well, have you ever gotten a whiff of hot French fries? What do you do? Head for the nearest What-a- Burger, right? Or have you ever been passed on the street by someone wearing the same cologne or perfume as your ex? What does *that* do to your brain? Conjure up powerful memories, right? This is what our senses do: they evoke emotions and memories. They create a mood. A good salesperson realizes this and *uses* it not just to sell a product, but to influence the experience.

Here's an odd one, but a powerful one: the smell of a new car. There's nothing like it. What you are actually smelling are just the chemical smells that come from the manufacturing and installation of plastic, fabric, and leather. Or ... is there something more? Isn't your new car also associated with excitement, pride, and success?

Our senses change our perceptions: they influence us and our decisions. They are of great *value* to the venture of selling.

Perceptions of Value – What Is value?

When we're selling, what we're really doing is making the argument that *something* – a product, a service, a person – has value. The perception of value is enormously powerful. It is a tool, and it should be used carefully.

But first, what is value?

The Oxford Dictionary defines value as: "The regard that something is held to deserve; the importance, worth, or usefulness of something." Value – this concept of what something is worth – also can influence and shift our perception. To be clear, this does not mean the price of a good. What we're talking about is the *perception* of that price.

Consider real estate. While pricing real estate may be tricky, for a consumer there are guard rails that can be used to create an estimation of value: There is data on inventory; there are comparable houses and their prices; and there are other factors, like location, which may make the price of a specific house *seem* to be a good or a bad deal. But even with such hard data, there is the "X" value of perception and that is very large indeed. It is also very malleable. Ask any realtor: oftentimes, the hard data flies out the window with the first view of the house or the first step inside the door. Love at first sight (perception) is a powerful thing.

Here's another example: Art. How does one value art? There are millions of artists out there, but one painting is on the market for $100 and this other hot mess is on the market for $1,000,000! The difference is in the perception of that painting's value. Both might be made of canvas and paint, but our *perception* of which is more valuable is going to be shifted by the intangibles of society, provenance, influence, and scarcity, with a nod to beauty, taste, and maybe even how it will look over your couch!

Valuation is hard.

Assessing the value of a home is tough. Assessing the value of art ... even worse. But assessing the value of a diamond? That's wicked hard!

It is in the glittering world of diamonds that perception reigns supreme. Yes, there are the 4 Cs of cut, clarity, color, and carat weight. They help. But when you're talking about diamonds, there's so much more. Learning from the industry can only teach you some of what you need to know. If you really want to understand diamonds, you need to dig into psychology.

Diamonds are not just sparkling rocks: they're crystallized dreams. They're the ultimate accessory. They're a symbol of love, yes, but also a demonstration of *how much* love! They signal great wealth and, through that, great power.

And it all comes down to perception.

Think about it: why will we willingly shell out a small fortune for a shiny piece of compressed carbon? Is it because diamonds are exceptionally rare? Nope. Diamonds aren't that rare. In fact, they're the most common gemstones on earth. What you're seeing in the price of a diamond is the work of a cunning illusionist – the diamond industry – which has created the perceptions of scarcity and beauty and luxury and power in the little shiny rocks we know as diamonds. Genius, really.

Consider the drama and angst surrounding the engagement ring. There's some poor soul, standing nervously over a shiny display case in a jewelry store, eyeing the rows of rings, trying to figure out *why* he's about to drop three months of his salary on that little, tiny rock. But there he is. It's an unwritten rule.

"Not to worry ... we offer financing!"

We all know that the size of the rock isn't proportional to the success of the marriage. But society has made the commitment of marriage a material thing. It's the ultimate manipulation of perception.

The diamond industry didn't stop at scarcity: they threw in the idea that bigger is better, too. Suddenly, a modest diamond won't do. Nope. It must be a statement piece – a tangible measure of your love's grandeur. And don't get me started on the whole "diamonds are forever" spiel, unless you're referencing a Bond movie. Sure, diamonds are durable, but so is a good, sturdy relationship, and you don't need a shiny rock to prove it. Diamonds aren't relationship wizards. They're just tools of the diamond industry at its marketing finest.

Perception. Do not underestimate.

What's the takeaway from this dazzling display of perception acrobatics? What we perceive as real is often a carefully crafted illusion. That sweet, yet musky, aroma in the men's store isn't just to cover up something; it's to entice you to purchase the cologne. Personally, I appreciate smelling good. To me, receiving a compliment about how nice I smell completely justifies the purchase. I mean who doesn't like the attention? That diamond on your finger isn't just a rock; it's a testament to your partner's commitment.

How we perceive things is powerful.

So, how can you play the perception game? How can you influence the decisions, actions, and reactions of others? How can you sell the next $1,000,000 painting? Or the next diamond?

It's all about unraveling the mystery of the mind. Perception is like a magician's trick. It's the art of creating an experience that resonates with the audience long after the curtain falls.

In the realm of marketing, whether you're selling a product, a service, or even yourself, consider the power of perception. What visual, auditory, or olfactory cues can you strategically incorporate to create a memorable experience? Be attentive to the emotions you're trying to create. Do you want to evoke desire, comfort, adventure, or even, perhaps, excitement? Remember, it's not just about the product: it's about the story you're telling and the emotions you're evoking.

People Perceptions

Let's now look into the world of personal branding. In that world, you are your own product, my friend. How you present yourself—the way you dress, speak, and carry yourself—is all part of the perception game. Are you the casual, approachable, flannel-wearing buddy or the sleek, professional expert with funny named shoes? Your choice shapes the perception others have of you.

Ever watch politicians give a speech? They are not only reading a script: they actually have been coached on how to deliver that speech and *sell you* on their message, their policy, their vision ... them.

Ultimately, politicians are candidates. What they're selling is the perception that they are just what you, your community, your state, your country needs.

Now, imagine you're in a job interview. You've aced the qualifications, but what kind of impression are you making? What perception does the interviewer have of you? Are you showcasing confidence, competence, and a sprinkle of Charisma? *(No, not the stripper from New Orleans)*. Remember, it's not just about what you say or write; it's also about how you say it, the non-verbal cues you give, and the overall experience you leave behind.

TIP: The value of an employee lies much more in the perception of what that person brings to the table than it does in their resume. Employers have hundreds of resumes. They don't need another qualified applicant – they need a person they think will vibe with the company's work environment, will generate positivity, is creative, and an achiever. Most employers know that they can teach an employee to do the job. -

What they can't do is give you the drive and personality that will work for them. And neither one of those will fit on a resume – they must be perceived by an employer, who sees a candidate confidently hold forth, engage with others, and project their value. It's not an entry on a resume that wins over an employer ... it's their perception of you.

The Fine Details of Perception

In the grand theater of perception, colors, fonts, and even the layout of a webpage – even how I lay out this book – play starring roles. Ever wonder why some websites feel more trustworthy than others? It's not just the content: it's the perception they cultivate. Warm colors, clean design, and user-friendly interfaces create an experience that says, "Hey, you can trust us." These are not those websites full of exclamation points or crammed with unnecessary text shouts or are full of promised value or unlimited discounts.

Discounts – "But It's on SALE!"

Let's look at another approach to the perception of value.

What if I told you that the very gorgeous, very shiny, *cooler-than-you-really-are,* must-have watch that all the Navy Seals wear was now *on sale*? What would your reaction be?

Discounts, the heat-seeking wallet missile!

Price is a silent seller. Silent selling is used to entice us by unspoken suggestions which grab our attention. A silent selling technique might be *how* the price of an item is presented to you (**70% off!**). It might be *where* you place the item (shelf placement). It might be its convenience for the buyer (right up next to the cash register).

Ever seen a fancy-looking bottle of liquor on the top shelf of a bar? It must be the best to be next to the other expensive brands, right? Nope. The bar owner just hopes you think that. Its *placement* sold you on its unknown quality.

Or, what about that new car roped off inside a dealership? Don't touch! It's special! Right? Sure. It's special because it's green and that's different from the other 40 cars outside.

But it's the silent seller of value that has the most impact, day in and day out. Throw a *"Drink Special"* or a red **"SALE"** sign on it, and we immediately begin to think differently.

Why do we gravitate to what might be on sale? What is it about the notion of getting more value that is such a powerful sales motivator? I think it's because we've been programmed to think that if we purchase something on sale, we are winning.

Q: Ever get that online pop-up coupon with "just-for-you special code"? **"SAVE 30% with Promo Code X"**

Q: Ever act because the deal you've been offered is **"Expiring"?**

Q: Have you ever been told, **"Hold on for a minute. Let me speak to my manager and see what we can do"?**

That last one is my favorite. Sure, I'd love to sit here and wait for you to make a fake trip to the back room.

Saving the customer money is rarely a company's motivation behind these kinds of sales tactics. Instead, special coupon codes, expiring sales prices, and the 'Let me speak to my manager" ploy are all simply sales tactics that create the perception that you're scoring a deal. They create the perception that you're saving money ... and winning.

What you should understand, as a salesperson, is that such approaches are remarkably successful.

What you should understand, as a consumer, is that the business model of the retail shop you are in with all of the huge discounts is oriented around volume selling.

"Everything 70% Off!"

But, what if instead you say, "Everything is $19.99!"

Each of those invokes a different reaction. But consider this: both are for the same item, and both represent the same price in the end.

To make the sale, you must create a perception of *value*. A high price at a discount might feel like a deal to consumers. Conversely, a low price might convey the perception of a low quality.

~

In the end, using perception is all about crafting experiences that stick in the minds of your audience. It's about understanding the psychological nuances that influence decision-making. Once you understand how to use perception as a tool, you'll be able to apply it to almost every situation – both in business and in your personal life. Never forget: The perception of the value of what is being offered is paramount to consumers, employers, even in your relationships.

Whether you're a marketer, a job seeker, or someone navigating the intricate dance of personal relationships, remember this: perception isn't just a spectator sport; it's a game you can control and master.

Chapter 2: Microdose Marketing

Alright, gather 'round as we venture into the mind-bending matrix of microdose marketing. No, we aren't talking about party 'shrooms here. We are talking about a clandestine dance of persuasion that unfolds before our very eyes in tiny ways. In this chapter, we'll unravel the mysteries of how subtle marketing maneuvers can leave an indelible mark on our minds, and guide our preferences, decisions, and, dare I say it, our wallets.

Let's kick this off with a revelation that may ruffle a few feathers. Microdose marketing begins with you, because believe it or not you are a product. Yes, you heard it right. From the way you style your hair to the scent you choose to wear; every detail is a brushstroke on the canvas of your personal brand. And just like any product on the market, your visual appeal sends a little message to the world—a message that influences opinions, perceptions, and your success as a salesperson.

Every action you take – whether large or small – influences your surroundings and the people in them. That means, you *must* sweat the small stuff (again!). It also means that you don't have to hit consumers over the head with a Sale or a Discount or a bunch of exclamation marks. What I am talking about is microdose marketing: the deliberate and strategic marketing that is also subtle, quiet, and incredibly effective.

What I need you to do now is to back away from that world of commerce where products dance on the stage of consumer attention; where they shout, dazzle, and ... sometimes undermine their own value. This is not the "louder is better" kind of marketing. Rather, microdose marketing is a special type of storytelling, one that hints at a lifestyle, a dream, a possibility.

Microdose marketing is about planting little seeds that, if planted correctly, will grow into big sales.

Ever scroll through your feed and suddenly find yourself hypnotized by the story being told on the screen? No one is selling anything, but all of a sudden you begin to smell the leather of a new luxury bag on your arm ... or crave freshly baked cookies. As you watch, the influencer on your screen – who is clearly enjoying life – talks to you about how great it was to visit Paris.

Now, there is no way you're going to visit Paris any time soon, but she seems to be happy and leading a full life with a lot of excitement and, by the way, she looks very chic. Maybe you can't visit Paris, but you want that travel-filled life – you *should have* that life —so you continue to watch.

Effortlessly, she weaves her story around this incredible adventure exploring the best eateries. But what holds your attention is *not* her story about her meal at La Tour d'Argent – whatever that is – it is the elegant leather handbag that she gently removes from her arm and sets on the table in front of her.

That is what you are being sold. And that is what has transfixed you. That influencer, babbling about Paris in her soft voice, has successfully introduced micro-dose marketing into her account of a trip you will never go on. It's not an overt sales pitch: it's a subtle invitation to envision your life intertwined with that product. Chic, exciting, exotic. Before you know it, you're imagining how that handbag – or sleek sunglasses or shoes or fine whiskey (for you guy readers) – could seamlessly fit into your world. It's microdose marketing at its finest—a gentle whisper that nudges you towards a purchase, a swipe, or a "Like" button smash.

Influencers. Tik Tok. YouTube. Facebook. Instagram. Instead of taking out a billboard or magazine ad, now you can advertise to billions of viewers around the world ... from your couch. Mainstream entertainment is now watched by everyone with a phone (which is everyone), and you can reach them all. And you can do so with exclamation points, or with sublime subtlety.

Since the creation of the internet, the dazzling entrepreneurial spirit of innovators and storytellers around the world has been seen on screens worldwide. That same spirit has sold us all millions of products. Billions of products. "Going viral" is now a good thing!

Microdose marketing – the repeated and subtle placement of products to influence and drive sales – tops the list of the most successful, entrepreneurial ways to influence people's buying choices.

Your thoughts are now running faster than a squirrel on meth crossing an intersection and you're hooked. You continue watching as this 'chef' in a thong, Jessica, stirs in the magic seasoning, and ... hmmm, you begin to wonder. *What the hell am I actually watching ... ?*

Oh ... It's a post about seasoning. Nice. Oh, and there's a little link to buy down there...

"CLICK"

Ah, social media.

Let's go through that story a little deeper: If I asked you what made you buy that seasoning, would you say it was Jessica in her bikini? Ummm ... maybe? But maybe not. Tough to say. But if I were to ask you what made you stop and watch that little scene? It was definitely Jessica. In the next chapter, I will talk more about how sexy sells; the point here is not that it sells, but that discovery is essential – unless viewers stop and watch your video, they will never know about your product. Viewers can swipe or scroll through multiple posts within seconds! I mean fast! So, you need to understand how to operate under those conditions. You've got a nanosecond to get them to stop, look at your visual, and then ... CLICK to learn more. You need something that will, in the blink of an eye, make them pause and click. It comes down to one of two things, visual appeal or entertainment value.

How Jessica used her visual appeal to sell-in this new bacon seasoning was one visually appealing way to promote that product without the billboard effect or bold logos. It was a "micro" way of advertising. When you do this with a bit of regularity, you are planting little hidden bombs that perhaps will trigger some other guy scrolling through his feed at 10 PM to CLICK.

Creating stark visual appeal or entertainment value to get readers to pause and CLICK has been studied at length and is now strategically used in almost every industry. It doesn't just work for social media either; step inside almost any retail store and you will see it in action. Have you ever wondered why certain products are in the window or strategically placed at eye level on store shelves? It's not a coincidence; it's by design and intended to influence your attention and choices in the same way that Jessica got you to CLICK on her *Bacon Flavored Jellyfish* post.

Take a look around. In stores, kids' toys are down low and adult items are up high. This, too, is microdose marketing. A product's visual real estate has an immense impact on a consumer and his choices, so much so that some vendors will pay for their products to be placed in a prime location in a store.

True story here: while working in the beer industry, I learned that some larger brands would buy out smaller brands just so they can take over more shelf space. Now, that's certainly an extreme, but remember it's not always a popularity contest; sometimes it's a visual presence game. The more often you see a product on a shelf when you pass by, the greater the chances you will reach for that product.

It's online, too: If your product pops up on the first page of the search results, it 100% has an impact on the clicks and likes and sales that product gets. This is because those products at the top of the search get more traffic. This is online product placement. How do products get to the top of the page? It's pretty simple: for many bucks, you too can be the top, sole, premier, and #1 website someone is looking for too! Whether online or in-store, prime placement comes with a hefty cost not all can afford ... but all would like.

Again, big bold advertising works, to an extent, with big brand names, but selling in a convenient, subtle, relatable, and entertaining way can have a lasting impact and influence. However, microdose marketing isn't just about hiding products in plain sight: Sometimes it's about trust.

A Face You Can Trust

Ever find yourself swayed by the products endorsed by your favorite actor, athlete, or musician? You're not alone. The psychology behind celebrity endorsements is a fascinating study about influence. When a beloved – trusted – celebrity aligns with a product, it's like a golden stamp of approval. Your brain subconsciously thinks, "If it's good enough for him (or her), it's good enough for me." Or "If they use X, then surely it's the best."

Celebrity endorsements are a shortcut for our minds; they help us make decisions in a world inundated with choices. In reality, celebrity-endorsed products may not be the best products available, but the presumptive thought process is: *"Because 'they' use them, they* must *be the best. Right?"*

This kind of microdose marketing is remarkably successful. However, microdose marketing isn't confined to traditional channels, like celebrity endorsements. That's pretty basic. Marketing 101. Look a little deeper. Think of the endless uses of products in film and tv. Just like the internet, old school media is great for subtle brand placements.

Product Placement

Picture this: a movie character, amidst a gripping action sequence, pulls out a sleek smartphone, showcasing its durability and reliability. It's not just a prop; it's a strategic product placement, planting the seed that this phone can withstand even the most intense of situations. Before you know it, you're considering that very phone for your next upgrade.

What we are talking about is product placement. In these marketing situations, products aren't just props: they've been placed in a situation where that same product is a hero. This is commercial product placement, another form of microdose marketing. The art lies in making you feel like you're not being sold a product, but rather you are being shown through entertainment a product you can relate to and envision using.

Some major brands out there sign deals with film studios or television producers to have their product involved in a movie or TV show, such as the use of a car brand, clothing, watch, even beverages.

Remember, branding can be done subtly and without words. It happens more than you think, as advertisements strategically feature people smiling, laughing, and enjoying life to the fullest. It's not always just about the product; it's also about the emotions they want you to associate with that product.

TIP: Like microdose marketing, happiness is socially attractive – others gravitate to it. Relax a little, surround yourself with positive and supportive people, and you will naturally be less stressed, approachable, and influential. Happiness sells itself, and it can help sell you.

Make It Quick. Keep It Short.

Our brains, much like easily distracted toddlers, thrive on constant change, color explosions, and captivating tones. Ever wonder why children's shows, movies, and even apps like TikTok are designed with a kaleidoscope of colors and rapid scene changes? It's all about keeping their viewers' brains engaged, stimulated, and, most importantly, hooked.

Social media works the same way. It keeps the viewer engaged by allowing them to quickly move through visuals and storytelling. According to one source, the average human attention span is just over 8 seconds. I'd say even less, depending on age. Successful internet marketing and advertising uses that knowledge wisely. They keep the content and the message short, engaging, and fast. They get your attention quickly and then strike just as fast.

Beyond social posts or online ads, product *packaging* works the same way. Creative product packaging can transform that lightspeed glance into a purchase. Like

Bacon Flavored Jellyfish clickbait, most products don't just sit on the shelf and wait for you: they beckon, they call out, they practically wink at you. It's the visual sensation of colors and displays that captures your attention and refuses to let go. Before you know it, that vibrant package of cereal is in your shopping cart, whispering promises of a delightful sugar-high experience.

Finally, let's throw a dash of humor into the mix. Imagine a world where products have personalities, and they engage in sitcom-style banter. Picture a hot dog cracking jokes about its buns or a body wash boasting about its tickling superpowers. Humorous twists add layers of relatability to inanimate objects. Humor can make a product feel like a friendly companion, rather than something to be stored in a cupboard under the sink.

In the grand tapestry of microdose marketing, the key is to understand that every visual, auditory, or olfactory cue is a note in the symphony of influence. Whether it's the strategically placed product in a store, the seamlessly integrated social media post, or the celebrity-endorsed commercial, each element is still another brushstroke in the masterpiece of persuasion and perception.

As we wrap up this chapter, let's raise a toast to the unsung heroes of microdose marketing: the architects of subtle persuasion, the magicians of in-store marketing, and the social media wizards who make us believe in the magic of a well-told story.

Chapter 3: Sexy Sells

Well, hey there *(wink wink)*; strap in as we embark on a whirlwind, and perhaps awkward, adventure into the mysterious realm of attraction by design. For those not in the marketing world or new to it, we're surprise popping the balloon of the world of sexy— where looks are the currency and visuals are the click bait that set-up the rendezvous between you and that oh-so- desirable product.

No matter if you are an advertising professional, a salesperson, or on a date, this form of marketing is no stranger, literally, to anyone.

Let's start this spicy journey with a truth bomb: Sex sells. (In my dark, caped superhero voice: "Like a lot.") It's not a mere coincidence that some of the most memorable advertisements feature barely clothed models, "take me" stares, or a seductive aura that would make a nun sweat. Whether it's a perfume ad or a car commercial, the underlying message is clear: buy this, and you, too, will captivate all who see you.

Serious Caveat: I've never understood a single perfume commercial or what scent they were selling. Ever. For me, all someone would have to do is tell me, "Hey, wear this scent and you will get compliments all the time!" I'd buy that product 100x over the product whose commercial features the heavy breathing beach-prancing dude.

The secret of how to appeal to the masses lies within, yet again, perception. But in this discussion, we're going to throw in a little desire. Everyone believes they have a special feature – it could be their body, their hair, their sense of humor, even their voice. You should embrace what you believe makes you, YOU. Once you are comfortable with 'you,' self-confidence will follow. That alone will make you stand out and give you 'presence.'.

***TIP:** Confidence in yourself is a valuable asset, but keep in mind, there is a difference between confidence and cockiness. It's all in your delivery. Bringing confidence gives confidence.*

One way that advertisers give a product presence, since it's tough to give products a charismatic personality, is to design them specifically to be sexy. Take a glossy candy red sports car with curvy hips over the back wheels, clean body lines, and a parked stance that looks like 14 speeding violations. Sexy? I think so. And it was meant to appeal to me. But it's all an opinion. Some might prefer a rough, off-road warrior, but they should know that it, too, was designed to appeal to a specific customer.

The term sexiness to many involves physical features. Product designers use this construct to make their products appeal, to make them sexy. Take the whole actual "SEX" part out of this. "SEXY" has a whole other meaning. When you seek to make a product sexy, you are looking to evoke an emotion ... and you are almost always talking about visuals. I believe that you can actually make any product sexy. To do so, you must understand who your audience is, what they would find visually appealing, and what aspect of your product might trigger that emotion.

SEXY = Visual Appeal, NOT Sex.

In every situation or product you are selling, be strategic. Figure out how to present it as visually appealing as possible. To do that, ask, *Is this what my target audience will find easy on the eyes?* Your product doesn't have to have long legs or a sharp jawline; you can make *anything* appealing by the use of colors, overall shape, materials, and even convenience. And if you feel you have the least "sexy" product on earth, all you have to do is market, package, and present it differently – better – than your competition.

An easy example of an everyday product that was reimagined to be sexy is the old-fashioned fountain pen. Today, a nice pen is a tiny accessory that exudes professionalism, old school wealth, highbrow taste, and high-power success. The glossy black pen with its gold accents or touches of precious gems has a commanding weight. Just holding it draws forth a reaction. It's tough to pinpoint, but this pen is NICE! With its subtle curves and sleek look, it is, yes, ever so slightly sexy.

TIP: *Never leave that pen on your desk or counter. It will be swiped.*

Ohhh! Click ME …

So, here is where we actually start talking about physical attractiveness in the sexual tense.

An easy example for the younger social media addicts: picture this, you're scrolling through your social media feed, innocently looking for the latest offensive meme, when all the sudden, "BA-BAM!" An image of an impossibly attractive individual hits those lower feels. It's not just click bait; it's click-and-swoon. The power of physical allure is harnessed to make you stop, stare, and, more importantly, engage with whatever product or content lies beneath that perfectly crafted facade.

Remember Jessica and the *Bacon Flavored Jellyfish*? Yeah, I was totally interested in whatever she was making and that's why I clicked. "Clickbait?" More like "click-hook, line, and sinker."

In the realm of social media, where attention spans rival that of a person with ADHD on caffeine, attraction is the secret sauce. Whether it's the perfectly contoured jawline of a male model, solid abs, or the effortlessly curled hair of a female influencer, social media marketing is a carefully choreographed dance to make you like, share, and, ideally, buy whatever they're peddling. The presumption the influencer is counting on is that the viewer will believe that using the same makeup, hairbrush, straightener, or mascara will make them look equally hot.

We shouldn't be too harsh on ourselves; after all, we're all drawn to the allure of aesthetic appeal. From the moment we step into a social gathering, our brains are playing a never-ending game of "Who's the Attractive One?" It's not shallow; it's survival of the fittest—or, in this case, survival of the most beautiful. We're wired to be drawn to beauty like moths to a flame, and that's not necessarily a bad thing.

But attraction is a personal opinion and comes in all shapes, sizes, colors, flavors, and sounds. What you like might be the complete opposite for someone else. Sexy doesn't discriminate. Sexiness could be your ability to make someone smile or laugh! Let's take a moment to appreciate the power of first impressions. Research tells us that we form judgments about people within milliseconds of meeting them. That's faster than it takes to heat up your leftover pizza. So, whether you're going for a job interview or a first date, your appearance, body language, even your choice of pizza toppings, play a pivotal role in shaping that lightning-fast judgment.

***TIP:** Men and women statistically are more attracted to a personality than they are to your gym game or how many layers of caked-on makeup you put on to look like a viral TikTok chick with a gluten intolerance. Present yourself with a personality. Your personality is what's most winning.*

Viral Fiber

Now, let's push our shopping cart into the isle of brands and their cunning use of physical attractiveness. Let's take a fashion ad where we see an attractive, skinny female rocking the latest indie trend, and all we catch is that she is using fiber to obtain that small physique. It's simple: all you need to be hot and trendy is just a warm glass of fiber once a day.

WTF!

That cannot be. But yes, it's true: even fiber can go viral. The product in question has cleverly manipulated your desire to be associated with beauty and glamor.

This is all in the marketing of sex appeal. By showcasing models who look like they descended straight out of a bikini catalog, brands create an aspirational allure—a promise that, by wearing their clothes or using their products, you too can ascend to the realm of the godly gorgeous, which means, of course, being digestively regular.

FIBER
Li'l Edition
It keeps you regular.

It's funny how we view attraction here in the U.S. In other countries, attractiveness might be a full round belly, a long neck, or even just those enchanting eyes hidden behind a veil. Each culture has a different take on attraction and adjusts its marketing to each. Selling a product, yourself, or even a concept, you must first know your audience, and then appeal to them. Remember, sexiness doesn't only mean showing some skin. Knowing how to engage your audience is key, because different audiences will have different ideas about sexiness and physical attraction.

So, what else besides overt, physical beauty can be sexy? Never forget the power of body language. A well-timed glance, a playful smile, or even a subtle hair flip—these are the secret handshakes of attraction. We will get more into this later in Chapter 5, but brands understand this language and employ it with the finesse of a Casanova at a masquerade ball. The models in their ads aren't just displaying products; they're engaging in a flirtatious tango with your subconscious, whispering, "This could be you and me. Just buy what I'm selling."

Let's inject a dose of humor into this intoxicating mix. We should not forget the flip side of this captivating coin. Sometimes a product isn't socially or physically attractive, in these situations, humor can take center stage. Imagine a world where products have dating profiles like the hot dogs and body wash in Chapter 2, which come complete with witty taglines and profile pictures, like a perfume bottle boasting about its "Smell of Success" or even toilet paper that promotes "Swipe back, not right." These are hilarious twists that remind us not to take the game of attraction too seriously. Sometimes, the use of humor can be memorable and attractive.

In our real-life quest for attractiveness, we often stumble into the realm of overthinking. From agonizing over the perfect outfit to dissecting the ideal angle for a selfie, we sometimes forget that true allure lies in authenticity. Brands are guilty of this too; they occasionally overdo the glamor, making us wonder if the model in the ad is even a real human or whether she's an AI creation.

Random two cents: *For God's sake, can we not sell perfume without making a commercial a mini drama? Also ... why do we see stick figure models with 6 pack abs selling French fries?! You know for damn sure "Trevor" here doesn't eat French fries with his organic kelp tea.*

FRENCH FRIES

As we navigate the labyrinth of attraction, let's celebrate the beauty in imperfection, the allure in authenticity, and the fact that attractiveness is subjective. What one person finds irresistibly charming, another might not. Let's raise a glass to the simple truth that beauty, in all its forms, is a kaleidoscopic celebration of the human experience.

So, whether you're swiping right on a dating app or choosing a product from the shelves, trust your instincts, embrace your own unique charm, and remember that, in the grand spectacle of life, attractiveness is just one dazzling act in the weird carnival of existence.

Chapter 4: Be Quiet

Ah, my boisterous speakers, just be quiet and listen as we unravel the enigma of silence in the grand art of effective communication. In this chapter, we venture into the labyrinth of words unspoken and we explore how silence, wielded with the finesse of a maestro, can orchestrate victories in conversations, negotiations, and the intricate dance of influence.

It's the magic of strategic silence, my friends—a tool in the arsenal of those who understand that in the realm of communication, less can indeed be more. Being able to listen not only helps you process what is being said, but also shows restraint, respect, and allows more time to effectively contribute to the conversation.

Let's start our silent symphony with the power of words ... and no words. Now, don't get me wrong: words are the backbone of communication. But in the art of influence, it's not about the quantity; it's about the quality. Successful communicators understand the art of choosing words like a jeweler selects precious gems—each one with a purpose, each one contributing to the masterpiece.

Personal Story. Not about jewelry though.

When I was younger, I was an EMT and everyone said I should try car sales instead, because of my personality. Soon, I was hired to sell Hondas at a local dealership and learned that everyone hates a pushy car salesperson. So, instead of standing outside next to the buyers, like a circling shark, I would wait inside, let a customer park, get out, see where they were walking, and then *I'd wait a couple more minutes*. My waiting allowed me to gather the data I needed. That data told me everything: what kind of car they were there for, whom they were buying for, their favorite color car.

Also, I could usually pick out a topic with which to break the ice. (Were they wearing a team hat? Were they bundled up because of the weather? Did they look like newlyweds?) I would then grab the brochure of the particular vehicle that had caught their attention and take it out to them, introduce myself, let them know if they had any questions to please let me know. I would then take a few steps back to give them some space to themselves.

"Ba-BAM!"

In time, like clockwork, they would turn away from the car and toward me to ask their questions. My giving them their space was the hook!

The point here is that no one likes to be hustled or attacked, as most buyers assume the role of an introvert. Using silence in that situation made the buyers feel comfortable and gave them a sense of a low-tension environment.

Understanding that customers want space and low-pressure environments is a tool you can use to influence their overall impression and experience. This doesn't mean don't introduce yourself or ignore them, just don't hit them with everything you've got and force a conversation. Tone it down a little, observe, listen, and know when to jump in and when to be silent. Be inviting through the use of time, space, and silence.

Types of Silence

Positive silence can be used to listen, which shows respect and engagement with the speaker; it can also be used when presenting, to allow the listener to play a mental movie of your story. The use of positive silence can be very effective; those who use positive silence are often described as being 'good listeners.' Being a good listener shows the client you are invested in the conversation and in what they have to say. It also allows you to gather as much information as possible to effectively respond to their needs and questions. This is no small thing.

Listening is one of the best tools you have in your toolbox. Your customers want to be heard or your partner may need to vent. Listening can have a positive impact on the speaker *and* the situation. It's a talent that takes very little effort, but whose returns are great.

Negative silence can be like mental terrorism. Ever had or given someone the silent treatment? Being on the wrong side of the silent treatment is the worst. But, in the realm of negotiations, practicing negative silence can be an effective tool of leverage. In short, it's like saying you are holding all of the cards.

Consider real estate negotiations.

Story: One time, when I was looking for real estate, I found an investment property in a beautiful, yet remote, area. I did a ton of research on it prior to making an offer – I knew the pros and cons and had even used Zillow to tell me how many days the property had been on the market and how many views and saves it had, which let me know how it was performing and how I might best approach the offer.

Because of that research, I strategically put in a 'quick close, cash offer' for much less than asking on a Friday afternoon. As I felt my offer was reasonable, I told my realtor upfront, "I'm aggressive and not open to back-and-forth negotiating. My offer is what it is."

The seller came back, of course, with a higher counteroffer than mine, but I said to my realtor: no counteroffer. Just say, "No thank you."

Well, this left the seller and agent on a weekend in a spot of questioning, immersed in the fear of missing out (FOMO). Now, I'm playing the mental game of negative silence. I hold the golden ticket. Sure as a sunrise, that Monday rolled around, no other offers had magically appeared over the weekend, and the FOMO was just getting stronger. The seller's agent called my agent and wondered if I would be open to reconsideration still at my original offer.

By my use of this "silent game," I had made my intentions clear. I had also made clear the strength of my convictions about my perception of the property's value. It wasn't that I was trying to pressure the seller: rather, I had determined the value of the property to me, had made an offer, and then stood my ground. I was supported by the fact that my purchasing the property filled a desire, a want, not a need. Sellers need to understand that it's just business.

Either their price – to them – was firm, or it was negotiable. It is that simple. But that doesn't mean that there wasn't strategy involved: I used their fear of not receiving another offer to induce them into seeing my offer in a different light. In this situation, the seller had set a high price anticipating a negotiation, but ultimately felt that the price I offered was better than no offer at all. It wasn't long after I made my offer that the deal was sealed. My strategy here was to play on their FOMO through my use of negative silence.

This doesn't apply to all situations or deals, and definitely does not work in relationships – silence will kill any valued relationship. But in sales, sometimes the less said, the better.

There is a difference in using time to respond vs cutting someone off completely. *Never* ghost someone – it's the height of unprofessional. Strategic communication is a positive in every situation.

Let's take moment and go over some aspects of silence.

Caution (1): Speaking too quickly is like a speed-dating session where you barely catch a glimpse of the person before moving on to the next. In the realm of sales communication, rapid-fire delivery doesn't allow the listener's brain to visualize and create an emotional connection. It's like watching a movie on fast forward—a strobe light of scenes which never gives you a chance to create a reaction.

Caution (2): On the flip side, speaking too slowly can turn a conversation into quicksand. The listener's interest wanes, distractions sneak in, and, worst of all, there's room for interjections that can derail your carefully crafted narrative. It's like trying to dance the tango in slow motion —a recipe for awkwardness.

Now, let's delve into the auditory nuances that transform mere words into a symphony of persuasion. Picture a conversation as a musical composition, with highs, lows, and pauses—especially pauses. The strategic use of silence *is* the secret ingredient that will elevate a conversation or story from mundane to memorable. But when the silence is over, it's the TONE that you use which counts.

***TIP:** One of the most important things to learn, if not THE MOST IMPORTANT, in all of sales, is how to effectively communicate! Being the overly loud person that demands attention is annoying. Select the best moments to respond, share, and sell. Listen for your opportunity.*

Tone or TONE!

Let's take a moment to appreciate the beauty of tone modulation. Successful communicators aren't monotone automatons; they're vocal acrobats, traversing a spectrum of pitches, tones, and rhythms. It's not just about what you say, it's about *how* you say it. A great example is how lowering your tone at the end of a sentence can inject a sense of authority, making your words linger in the listener's mind.

TIP: *Master your tones and your message will always be received the way you intended.*

Almost every word can be construed differently just by the way we say it. Take the basic response: "Okay." Now, we can say it with an even, modulated voice. Or we can say it with enthusiasm. Or, we can say it with attitude. It's simple and easy to take even a basic word and make it exciting ... or toxic. The tone we choose can mean everything when communicating. Interjecting any amount of attitude, especially if you don't intend to, can come across as rude.

Tone modulation is one of the easiest, yet most overlooked, influences in communication. There's no trick.

Here's an experiment: Try, for one whole day, to respond to people in an upbeat and positive tone in every situation you are in. You'll have a great day and see the transfer of energy to those around you. No joke. Even if you come across a negative interaction, responding in a positive tone just might dissolve the negativity, lower the tension, and re-direct the future response. Yes, it's easier said than done, but the more you practice this, the more it will become natural. You'll see quantifiable positives from doing so.

Now, put your Crocs in sport mode, let's high knee skip into the realm of psychology. Our brains, marvelous contraptions that they are, thrive on the interplay of words and the spaces between them. Picture a well-constructed sentence as a series of puzzle pieces, with each pause representing a moment of suspense. A pause is an invitation for the listener's brain to fill in the gaps and to participate in the creation of meaning.

The ... Pause

Ever noticed how the most impactful statements are often followed by a pause? It's not a coincidence: it's a deliberate choice by the speaker to let his or her words sink in. This allows the listener to marinate in the weight of the message. In the grand theater of influence, silence is the stage on which the drama unfolds—a moment of stillness that leaves a lasting imprint. This interjection of silence brings more to your message than adding words.

Did you know that pausing in a conversation or just being quiet can help you maintain control of the situation? This trick is used all the way up to the world's leading military and political figures. Next time you see someone on TV addressing the press or a crowd, watch and listen for the pauses. When a speaker pauses, that pause not only gives the listener the time to process what is being said (and thus be engaged in the conversation) but can give the speaker a moment to help them read the person with whom they're speaking and then sculpt the direction of the next sentence.

Try pausing every now and then for 2 seconds when speaking or presenting, as if you're telling a story. Speak at a good rate, not slow and never fast. Doing so allows the listener to visualize what you are speaking about, process your words, and stay engaged. Now that you know this, you'll notice it during political speeches, with comedians, and more!

It is amazing what one can do with pauses and tones. Imagine a world where every sentence ends on an unexpected note, leaving people wondering if you're reciting Shakespeare or just giving directions to the nearest coffee shop. Modulating your voice – storytelling – gives a playful twist to your speech or conversation or presentation that will keep your audience on their toes.

__TIP__: Feel you might be losing the listener? To maintain attention, consider pausing your story, complementing them on something or themself. That pause stops the story, allows you to reach out and engage them, and allows you to 'reset' the situation and give it a positive foundation, at which point you pick the story back up. Be aware, however, that if you lost your listener the first time, you risk doing so again. You might consider fast-forwarding through the story or giving it up altogether and becoming the listener. Use positive silence. There will be a time to circle back and re-address.

Word Vomit

And now, my friends, let's touch upon the unpleasantness of "word vomiting." Picture this: you're in the midst of a riveting conversation, and suddenly, someone unleashes a torrent of words, drowning you in a verbal deluge. It's not just overwhelming; it's a huge turnoff. Word vomiting (aka speaking too much) is a surefire way to lose your audience. In the carnival of communication, it's essential to be a mindful conversationalist—know when to speak, when to listen, and when to not overdo it.

Even the best stories can be summarized into a shorter version. Doing so helps you hit the key points of the story, maintain engagement, and allows for reactions. Spilling all the beans and going into deep detail will not only cause you to lose your listener's attention, but it can also drag out a story unnecessarily (boring), risk you going off topic, and therefore risk losing the original intent of the story.

Effective communication isn't done through a lengthy speech or a novel-length presentation, it's done by expressing the narrative in a way that engages the reader in such a way that they form a response. And if you are strategically aiming for a specific response, you must keep it simple and engaging.

As we navigate this labyrinth of influence, let's not forget the cardinal rule about talking too much: never divulge all your secrets or the whole story. Whether in sales, negotiations, or the delicate dance of interpersonal relationships, leaving a little mystery is like sprinkling unicorn dust on your narrative. It invites curiosity, encourages self-cultivation, and ensures that your influence doesn't unravel like a poorly woven blanket from a flea market.

Instead, gather valuable information, listen to the unspoken cues, and respond with the finesse of a dance partner anticipating every step. Sometimes, having the person reiterate their thoughts can be a subtle dance move— a chance to reaffirm the emotional beats and show that you're not just a speaker, you're a partner in the conversion. Remember, you're a conductor orchestrating a symphony of understanding and influence.

I've been in many situations where I lost the listener during my storytelling or maybe never even had them in the first place. Super frustrating. But I used these experiences as data: I learned something from them – the person's areas of disinterest — and data is useful for a salesperson. Always.

TIP: I know you're super excited and your A.D.D. mind just thought of something, but don't interrupt someone. Let the spotlight circle the stage! It gets everyone engaged. I am notorious for this and am still learning control.

Not Sure How the Conversation Is Going?

Are they losing interest? Checking their watch? Checking the door? Here are some key words and phrases that may indicate disinterest or lack of engagement in a conversation:

"Ah."

"That's nice."

"Sure."

"I guess."

"Really." (In an incomplete sentence and non-question form)

"Mmm-hmm." (In a monotone voice and used repeatedly)

"Interesting." (Without genuine curiosity) (*Hate this one.*)

"I'll think about it." (With no follow-up) (*Ok. Sure. No, you won't.*)

"Yeah, you told me about that before."

"You think so?"

"I see."

"Neat."

Such responses likely signal a lack of interest or a desire to disengage from the conversation. Get out while you can.

Finally, there are the non-verbal cues: the lack of eye contact; your conversation partner is looking around the room or, worse, looking at their phone; or there seems to be an overall lack of engagement (their eyes seem a little glassy). These are all dead giveaways of a lack of interest.

RED FLAG! If someone responds with a negative response, even if the statement was positive, you should run. These types of personalities cannot get past negativity and are unable to positively contribute to the conversation. It's not you or your conversation; some people just think that way.

And now, my hopefully engaged reader, let's raise up a pint and give a metaphorical Cheers! to the unsung heroes of communication—those whose pauses are infused with possibility, who's carefully chosen words make the conversation interesting. The subtle influencers who understand that sometimes the most profound messages are the ones left unsaid.

Chapter 5: Ballet Of Body Language

Ladies, gentlemen, and cult members of the expressive arts degrees, step right up as we jazz dance into the enthralling realm of body language —a silent ballet that speaks volumes without uttering a single word.

Truthfully, there are actually experts out there who only study body language. They are frequently asked to provide analysis – and advice – on the communication skills of political figures and executives. They are tasked with explaining the gray areas of uncertainty, lies, truth, personal health, and more. Why? It's because it is very difficult to script posture, gestures, facial expressions, and physical reactions. Body language is a secret slide show of the subconscience. There's a lot to be said, even without words.

Subconsciously, our body reacts to situations naturally and automatically. This can lead to an observer making assumptions about the true nature of that person's reactions to whatever has been said. Being able to study, identify, and practice the art of body language can not only assist you in more effectively delivering your message, it can also allow you to set the scale, emotion and direction of the conversation. This part of psychology can be complicated, but in the upcoming sections we will touch base on a few hidden messages of body language and some that are literally an open book.

Body Language

Non-verbal cues, including body language and facial expressions, can significantly impact how individuals are perceived. Posture, gestures, and facial expressions can convey confidence and openness and genuine passion. They can also indicate deceit, disdain, and fear. Your body language is probably saying more about you than you realize.

In this chapter, we unravel the secrets of non-verbal communication, and explore how the sway of a hip, the arch of an eyebrow, or the subtlest of nods can narrate tales, paint emotions, and elevate the spoken word.

Consider you're on a dance floor: It is your body language that captivates the audience. We're not talking about a chaotic mosh pit; we're envisioning the presence of John Travolta doing his Saturday Night Fever thing – where each movement is deliberate, and each step is calculated to tell a story. It's not only entertaining, it's engaging.

TIP: *Reading body language is one of the hidden talents of successful salespeople and those men and women in the dating pool who always seem to have someone new on their arm. Take the time to learn more about body language; how to use it and how to read it.*

Let's kick off this disco by acknowledging that body language is not just a sideshow—it can be the main event. How you use your body when speaking should complement the message of your words. You should be orchestrating an ensemble of gestures, postures, and expressions.

When you find yourself in situations where you need to make an impact or create a strong impression, start to learn what you can do first *without words*.

Forming Visual Impressions

Eye Contact

Sustained eye contact can convey confidence, sincerity, and, most importantly, interest. Avoiding eye contact may suggest discomfort, shyness, dishonesty, or lack of interest. A blank and bold stare can be intimidating or show aggression.

Blinking Rapidly

Blinking rapidly can signal nervousness or discomfort. Of course, there are medical and environmental reasons for blinking, but there are also different types of blinking such as short and long blinks which can indicate something more in depth such as deep thinking or even a form of facial expression.

Facial Expressions

Facial expressions are a rich source of emotional cues. Smiles indicate happiness or friendliness naturally, while furrowed brows may signify confusion, concern, or displeasure. It is human nature to face each other while talking, so pay attention to the expressions you are seeing, and the stories they are telling.

Tip: Smile! Even if you feel you have a "resting grumpy face," crack that smile, even just a little bit! Smiles, in any size, make a person approachable and attractive.

Gestures

Hand movements and gestures can enhance communication. Open-handed gestures can convey openness and honesty, while closed fists or crossed arms may signal defensiveness or resistance. We use our hands and our arms in almost every situation. Be aware of what and how you are gesturing; are you doing so casually, or, in response to something? Caution: Be aware and don't flail about.

Posture

A straight posture often indicates confidence and attentiveness. Slouched or hunched postures may suggest disinterest or low energy. Keep your shoulders back when at all possible. Bonus: Doing so will help align your spine and improve your overall posture and comfort. Good posture is also a sign of self-awareness because it is a choice.

Crossed Arms

Crossing arms can signal defensiveness, disagreement, or discomfort. It may also be a way of creating a physical barrier, as if in distress. In other combinations, it can be a sign of projecting dominance, which is considered a power pose. Or it could simply be a sign that the person is concentrating. Two simple examples: First, it's hard to find someone with their arms crossed who is engaged in a funny or joy-filled conversation; second, if someone is sitting with their arms crossed, it is a solid signal that that person has some personal reservations.

Hands on the Hips

Some call this the "Superhero Pose." It's a pose that can indicate confidence, assertiveness, and readiness. One opposite of this is standing with your hands in your pockets, which can be a sign of nervousness, lower self-confidence, and even shyness. Don't think placing your hands on your hips is a sign of exhibiting authority or dominance, read it as a sign of engagement.

Leaning In or Out

Leaning in can signal interest and engagement, while leaning back or away may indicate a desire to create distance, disengagement, or loss of interest. You cannot influence either, but interest and suspense evoke a different reaction vs. say a vent session. When selling, you want to excite and engage, figure out what words might get them to learn off the seat as that's a physical sign of leverage. If you do see them sitting back, or leaning away, just imagine the conversation or situation as a "smell." If it's good, you lean in; if it is bad, you lean away.

Head Nodding

Nodding is generally a positive sign, indicating agreement, understanding, or approval. Excessive nodding, however, may be a sign of impatience and even at times conveying rote, passive agreement.

Head Shaking

Generally, head shaking suggests disagreement or disapproval. Also, it's the international sign for "no."

Mirroring

Mirroring involves mimicking the body language of the person you are interacting with. One can mirror another's posture, stance, or even gestures or motions. It often indicates rapport, connection, and empathy. It's a sign of listener engagement and is suggestive of the effects of your influence. You cannot deliberately generate this from your listener, but it can be a response in your own body language to project comfort, level of energy, or, sometimes, aggression.

Touch

Appropriate touch, like a handshake or pat on the back, can convey appreciation, warmth, and connection. In certain contexts, it may also indicate authority or dominance. Keep it simple, ethical, and only used when welcomed and appropriate.

Situational Sitting

While sitting, what you do with your legs may suggest a relaxed or laid-back attitude or it may also signal defensiveness or reservation. There's also a degree of appropriateness that must be heeded. There's a difference between crossing your legs to be comfortable and wearing a skin-baring mini skirt in a police interrogation room. Caution: your default way of sitting might be off-putting or inappropriate. Women: Try to choose your attire based on your most common body language and situation. If you are a natural leg crosser, you need to be aware of inadvertently showing too much 'you.' Men: Beware – the legs-wide- open posture is often seen as unprofessional and a sign of low interest.

Tapping or Fidgeting

Tapping your fingers or fidgeting can indicate impatience, nervousness, or restlessness. Or ... ADHD. Caffeine, too, can influence this. Don't read too much into this one. Yet, there are occasions when tapping or fidgeting can be a sign of a person's level of anxiety, a clear sign.

Micro-expressions

Micro-expressions are genuine, automatic physical expressions that reveal our true emotions. They're tremendously useful. They are also the type of body language that is most overlooked. Micro-expressions often occur involuntarily and can be very brief, such as a quick look down, a readjusting in the seat, or even a quick side grin. These are reactions to the conversation or situation and can be a sign as to the level of engagement. Some expressions are facial, while others are body movements. All are subtle.

Sign Language (sort of)

Hand Movements

The use of your hands can set and give scale. *(The fish was this BIG!)* It can also present a visual to the story you are telling. At times when speaking, the use of hand movements is a way to captivate and maintain the attention of the listener.

You can see this often when someone is presenting and they may bounce their hands in front of them, and in a lot of cases this is natural to them to use their hands.

On the other "hand" *(that felt like a dad joke ...),* learning some intentional hand gestures can express your message, set tones, be inviting, and even express authority ... or anger. No, we are not talking about the middle finger here; we are talking about adding small visuals to your audio book.

Your hands have a lot to say, much like sign language. Gesturing with your palms up can seem inviting and, when used directionally like lifting a box off the stage, you can "LIFT" not only the eyes of those around you, but your voice as well. Your palms are not only directing the eyes of your listeners, but you're actually opening up your lungs and vocal cords to lift your tone!

Palms down can suppress your natural tone and tend to lower your volume, allow you to change context, and, when in motion, even visually defuse conflict. Again, what you do with your hands can amplify your words, your tone, and your story.

To learn a little more on the effects of these hand signals, here are a few examples.

A Few Positive Uses of Hands When Speaking

Open palms: When speaking and having your hands out in front of you, with open palms and rolling of the wrist, this in the air sets an open scale, draws attention, and presents like a visual stimulant. It acts like you are handing out or presenting your words.

Flat hands: Speaking with hands flat and together pointing in the direction of the listeners can show assertiveness, belief, and be a sign of humbleness. It can be inviting and set a lower tension of the message.

Thumb pointing: When presenting a message with one hand out, like you were pointing with one finger, but curling it in front of and around your thumb nail. This one is very unique as only a few types of messages and personalities use this. When this is done, it doesn't have a purpose, but what it does is much like pointing like a matter of fact, but instead, it gives off a humble, deep thought or emotion, and not used in a negative situation.

A Few Negative Uses of Hands When Speaking

Often body language and hand cues are unmistakable when someone is under distress, but sometimes the use of the wrong gesture in the wrong situation can change the tone or engagement of the listener. You should always try to control your hands in these situations, as large gestures can escalate a bad situation and even be a sign of aggression.

Here are a few of those examples.

Flat hand out: Speaking with your hand out and palm down signals sternness and trying to solidify a point with visual weight, as if you were pushing or suppressing something down. Often a natural reaction to a conflict or strong point being made.

Towering: Typically, there is not a visual or expressive need to raise your hands above chest level. Although it's used in celebration or excitement, it can also be a sign of hostility and aggression if coupled with a louder tone. To the listener, this towering effect will cause them to withdraw and raise concern.

Pointing with one finger: Accusation, emphasis

Pointing with four fingers: Signals authority, dominance, frustration (aka "Chop Hand")

"Air Quoting" with Fingers: Expressing, mocking, demeaning.

Finger tapping: Impatience, anxiety, ADHD. Remember, interpreting body language is nuanced, and context is key.

The gestures and postures above are only a few of ways that non-verbal body language can convey your thoughts; your impressions of and receptivity to a conversation or presentation; your engagement and interest in the topic at hand; and your willingness to continue along the journey being presented. Keep in mind, everyone is different and interpreting body language requires context; variations of interpretation exist. People may display different cues based on cultural background, personality, medical conditions, and specific circumstances.

Also, it's often useful to consider a cluster of body language cues rather than relying on a single gesture or expression to accurately interpret someone's feelings or intentions. No two people are alike, but if you're alert to the possibility, you'll start to pick up what's going on *in their minds* by observing what they're doing with their body.

Setting SCALE without a word.

Finally, let's swan dance into the crucial concept of using body language to scale what you are saying. What do I mean by that? In a nutshell, I'm talking about the breadth and scope of your body's gestures. In the grand theater of body language, scale is the secret ingredient that adds depth and emphasis to your communication. Whether you're expressing joy or delivering a stern message, the *scale of your movements* sets the tone. A slight nod for agreement, a dramatic gesture for emphasis—it's all about finding the right scale for the emotional symphony you wish to conduct. And here comes the *pièce de résistance*—how you scale your physical engagement can directly impact the psychological engagement of your listener or audience.

When you're in a conversation, it's not only about the words exchanged; it's also about the unspoken dialogue happening beneath the surface. A smile, a sympathetic nod of the head, or the subtle mirroring of gestures—these are the silent agreements and the gestures of shared understanding that build rapport and create an unspoken connection.

When weaving a narrative, *successful* storytellers don't stand stiffly and deliver a monologue; nor do they throw words around like confetti. Successful storytellers weave their stories' rich tapestries using carefully chosen words and strategic tones. They pull in and embrace their audience with warm gestures and relatable moments.

It is through these carefully chosen words and gestures and tones and shared moments that a great storyteller will command the attention of the room and hold the spotlight. In the world of influence, it's not about bombarding your audience with information; it's about creating a mental movie—a vivid, engaging story that unfolds in the minds of the audience. Body language is *integral* to the success of storytelling.

***TIP:** Try sharing a story with these physical cues: Put on a light smile, and, with one or both hands, reach out halfway and mid-level toward the listener for a few seconds, and begin your story that way. It's as if you're physically bringing them into the story. This draws their attention to you and engages their imagination.*

Meet every situation with inviting and choreographed body language. Afterall, sales is a presentation. Win that Oscar!

Chapter 6: Judgemental

Don't be judgy, because in today's world people are WAY too judgmental.

We all have seen someone walk through the door all branded up, cocky stride, chin high, and, you guessed it, they're not on the latest A list or B list or even the C-List. But they wanted to give off the perception they were. What would your first impression be?

It's human nature to judge. We do so almost instantly. And sometimes that judgment is nasty and mean-spirited, and sometimes it is just an instinctive reaction. Either way, judgment is a reality we all contend with – in that we both judge and are judged. It is important for a successful salesman to be aware of both sides of the coin. And also, to take the extra steps to put yourself in the best light you can.

In today's society, trends set the bar on status and looks, and even impact our personalities. We often let society dictate our choices of what we drive, where we live, or what we post. When we let society intrude on our decisions like this, we are essentially trying to manipulate how others see us. We are trying to ensure a certain type of perception. But there is a huge caveat to this scenario: What one person has accomplished, possesses, or knows is not always worn on their sleeve, advertised, or spoken of. Someone could wear expensive brand names from head to toe but be struggling with bills. Another person might have all the fame and money ever needed but suffer from loneliness. The truth here is that because we mainly judge people by what we *see*, the odds are high that unless we dig deeper, unless we take the time to get to know them, we will never really know who they are.

***Personal Note**: Don't ever judge people by their looks or what they're wearing. These days, I actively try not to be over the top name brand or blinged out ... but that came with maturity. When I was younger, I 100% tried to look and act beyond my means – a real douche move, I understand now. I remember growing up knowing old ranchers in old jeans with a pearl snap shirt but who had a gold Rolex under their sleeves. These guys didn't show off, but I knew they had helicopters. Now, on the other hand, I know guys with Rolex watches who can't afford their 18% interest used car loans. Little secret here: You never know what someone has going on. Never judge.*

What Is Being Judged?

Your Presence

It's no surprise that the top aspect people judge is your presence. It's sad and humbling to think that our looks are key to someone's opinion about us. But that's the reality. The fact of the matter is that, yes, how you present yourself is how society judges you. In the office or on a date, being aware of how you present yourself can only help guide people's opinions about you. You do not need the luxury brand or supercar, all you need is to embrace yourself, be authentic, be truthful, and carry yourself fitting to the environment you are within.

Communication Skills

How individuals express themselves – the words they choose, their skill in delivery, the rate of their speech, and their ability to focus on the message – has more of an impact on us than fancy, shiny things and PowerPoints. Clear and effective communication is a winning combination that allows you to share your message across social ecosystems. It also goes a long way toward making a strong impression. So, take your time, order your thoughts, modulate your speech, and speak confidently. Your communication skills are paramount: if you want to improve just onc thing, I'd 100% suggest that you master your communications skills. This is not about learning a ton of big, fancy, new words; it is about knowing what you want to say and how you want to say it. It is about communicating clearly and eloquently.

Some of the world's most successful people maintain that communicating well is the most important skill of a great leader. Those who do communicate well do so with the words they choose, the tones they use, and the quality of the context they share. Those who take the time to learn how to do this will be perceived as intelligent and approachable and will be less negatively judged.

Those who use inappropriate language, incorrect language, incomplete sentences, and the wrong tones will be judged negatively. And fast.

TIP: Keep a smooth tone and volume. You can fumble your words, but if you keep a good tone, don't rush, and use fewer words, your message will come across as intended.

Confidence

Confidence is both a psychological trait and a visual trait. A person who acts confidently and presents himself or herself with confidence draws in others. They generate charisma. *(No, still not the dancer from New Orleans.)* Appearing confident is simple: it starts with feeling comfortable with yourself. Not all confident people are extroverts and Type A personalities. Becoming comfortable in your own skin is a personal journey; it takes time to find your self-confidence. And self-confidence is known to be one of the hardest traits to acquire (and even harder these days, no thanks to social media or society's judgment scale). But a person with self-confidence, who believes in himself and is comfortable with himself, holds the world in his palm.

TIP: If you are trying to grow more self-confidence, practice this in front of the mirror: stand with your shoulders back and your chin level. Put your hands by your side (not in pockets) and look at yourself as you would people in the eye. The goal in doing this is to start to feel comfortable with how you see yourself in the mirror. Being comfortable with who you are is the first step toward becoming self-confident.

How someone carries themself, their level of self-assuredness, and their overall demeanor all contribute to the impression of confidence. This doesn't mean being loud and aggressive. Loud and aggressive are not confident. (They're just loud and aggressive – with a little obnoxious thrown in for good measure). There is something alluring about a person with quiet confidence, who feels no need to be loud. Learn to carry yourself with confidence. Figure out how you can show your own type of confidence, whether it be shoulders back, chin up, or pasting a big open smile on your face. Make it your trait and your personal standard.

TIP: Remember, there is a difference between confident and cocky. It's all in the execution. Be happy, humble, and inviting. Those few things are never construed negatively. I've made more friends, stood out more, and even been referred to as attractive because of my welcoming personality and my confidence in myself.

Personality Traits

Personality traits are just that: personal and singular to you. Your traits – your physicality, your attitude, your voice and style of speech, even your humor – can play a crucial role in how you are judged. Positive personality characteristics often contribute to favorable impressions. Your personality traits aren't trendy – they are your trademarks. Own them.

I should clarify that when I say personality traits, I mean everything about you that is unique to you. The world would be a truly boring place if we were all the same. Being different is a great thing!

TIP: Be yourself. There is not another like you in the world! Find your best self and shine. Reflect on yourself and ask how you can become a better version of yourself. Remember, tomorrow is another day! All you have to do is try to make it better than the one before.

It's important to note that your communications skills, your physical presentation, your confidence, and your kindness are interconnected. Certainly, as people get to know each other over time, deeper qualities like shared values, trustworthiness, and empathy become more significant in forming lasting impressions, but before that happens, you need to win people over with your first impressions.

Now, let's tango into the crucial territory of appropriateness. Successful communicators understand the fine line between expressive and excessive. Picture a conversation where every sentence is punctuated with wild gestures, as if you're conducting a symphony for an audience of one. It's not just distracting; it's a one-person show in danger of overshadowing the message. Your hands can tell stories by themselves, but they can also get you in trouble. Let's touch a little on that ...

The Power of Touch

A word of caution about the potential minefield of physical contact. While a well-timed hug can convey warmth and empathy, an unsolicited touch can be akin to stepping on a social landmine. Understanding what is appropriate and what veers into the realm of discomfort is crucial. Picture a scenario where your attempt at a friendly pat on the back is met with a virtual "danger" sign above the recipient's head. It's a humorous metaphor that underscores the importance of respecting personal boundaries.

Handshakes

Handshakes are about the only social and professional physical contact widely accepted. After all, it's a form of introduction, celebration, agreement, and exit. There is much to learn from a handshake. Strong. Weak. Clammy. Limp. Handshakes are not unlike fingerprints. And they are often judged. So, pay attention to how you shake hands.

Strong handshake: show of confidence, authority, acknowledgement, respect.

Overly strong handshake: projecting dominance, expression of control, authority, discontent.

Loose or limp handshake: Uncertain, nervous, lack of self-confidence. Keeping in mind that for the longest time, society thought it was normal for women to have a gentle, half handshake, and now we see more of the opposite. It's fantastic. I can't recommend a strong handshake enough ... for women and men.

Prolonging a handshake (2+ sec): Sign of comfort, interest tactic to make the other feel uncomfortable. There is another version of this too: it's a weird one where someone prolongs a handshake to assert dominance and control. In the end, whoever lets go first is the weaker or passive one. It's 100% awkward but I've seen it done.

TIP: When shaking someone's hand, meet their form of grip, match their strength, and release equally. This leaves little room for other impressions. Just make it simple and quick; there's no need to embrace each other.

In the grand finale of this body language ballet, let's raise a toast to the artistry of expression—the fluid movements, the silent dialogues, and the visual poetry that accompanies our spoken words. You can immediately capture a room with your body language, so take the time to practice this privately and create your own way of expressing your words through movement.

As I talked about body language in the previous chapter, first impressions and judgment can be perceived in many ways. Be sure to revisit this and the previous chapter a few times to home in on what you might be able to work on and also be able to recognize in others.

Shhh ... The carnival of non-verbal communication continues, and the ballet must go on!

Chapter 7: The Art of Selling

Welcome, my fellow lead singers of persuasion! Let's embark on a whimsical journey into the enchanting realm of salesmanship, where charm, wit, and a sprinkle of magic turn everyday encounters into opportunities to sell, sell, sell! You've gotten this far through this book; I hope it's all starting to come together for you. As we delve into the art of selling, remember the two golden rules:

Rule #1 – Everything is for sale. You just need to know how to package and deliver it.

Rule #2 — The #1 product you offer is yourself!

Not everyone has the same personality or drive, or skill set. Some people have a 'gift' for selling, others are natural presenters, still others have innate leadership talents. Everyone is different. As a society, we also tend to divide people into two different camps based on their personality:

There are people who shine in front of a crowd, and there are people who are more comfortable in the back of the room. We call these people extroverts and introverts, respectively. Each of these two different personalities has its advantages and disadvantages. Each can learn skills from the other.

For some, their extrovert personality allows them to freely speak and not mind new social interaction, whereas an introvert can be reserved, is more comfortable in known surroundings, and may choose to speak only when opportune. In sales, having an extrovert's personality has its advantages over that of an introvert, but it also comes with the need to know how and when to control the extrovert's outgoing nature. Talking too much, dominating the room, and constantly selling every situation are traps; none is flattering in social and professional settings.

For an introvert, being in sales is difficult. It is hard to reach out to new people (leads or customers), and tough as well to network or gladhand, all of which is part of the job. They won't drive people away with their outsize personality, but they will need to work on increasing their confidence in social settings. It is important to recognize your type of personality and understand both its strengths and drawbacks.

Story: *My folks told me when I was young, I used to try to sell them the Christmas gifts I handed them to open – most of which weren't from me! They loved that in me though. Even then I chased others reactions. Some people simply have the gift of the gab and are natural salespeople. I sell everything. I think part of it is the jolt I get from the chase and the reaction of the buyer. Even my kids will ask, "When are you going to keep something?" My response is always, "Well, you're still here. But that's because there was no return policy."*

The Pitch

Now, we know that selling is a delicate art, which is impacted by our storytelling, our communication skills, and our body language. You're trying to sell doo-hickies. How do you start?

"You stand tall with your head up and your arms open wide. You draw scale with your words and your hands. Your facial expressions bring climactic twists, and your body language starts the unfolding drama.

What am I describing?

It's the dynamic tale about the extraordinary value of the doo-hickies you are offering for sale. It's your sales pitch. Just as you wouldn't go on a date and try to seal the deal within minutes, you wouldn't do that on a sales call either. On a date, you need an opener. You need to build the relationship. There needs to be chemistry.

Ultimately, you are selling yourself. Here's the thing: Selling doo-hickies is exactly the same, but slightly more streamlined and the chemistry thing is slightly less fun.

Open a dialogue with a side topic to "break the ice." Then go to work. In sales, you must understand what the customer is looking for and why (what problem he is looking to solve), and either relate to him in some way (chemistry) or present the product you are selling as a solution. Neither of these scenarios requires a long-winded story: most don't care, so just keep it simple and relate.

Story: When I came out with the BevBuckle, which is a retractable can or bottle-holding belt buckle - as seen on TV – I had to get someone's attention fast, but with humor and in a way that allowed them to see themselves using it. So, by using short phrases like, "It's like Bluetooth for your beer" and showing how it worked, I got my point across within seconds. In marketing, can your imagery sell the product?

Below you will find a number of good steps that can serve as a field guide on bestselling techniques. But don't forget the power of a well-timed pause in your physical performance. Or the impact of a "Ba-BAM!" Or how the power of silence or a pregnant pause can amplify your message. Use these techniques wisely, and you'll have your listeners on the edge of their mental seats. And now, as promised, here are just a few simple methods to guide you in the art of selling.

Act 1: The Charm Offensive

Picture this: You walk into a room and heads turn, not because you're a celebrity (though you might feel like one), but because your smile is contagious. In the art of selling, charm is your secret weapon. Be the person everyone wants to talk to and buy from, not just because of the product but because they can't resist your Charisma. *(No, still not that extra friendly dancer from New Orleans.)* Charm is as easy as giving out a simple compliment, showcasing a smile, or even making someone laugh.

TIP: Fun tricks I've used that kicks off charm instantly, wear fun socks, a funky bow tie, or perhaps bold glasses. All of these give off a fun vibe which is always welcoming and unforgettable. Even if this isn't you, it works. Just have fun and try it. The days of the boring suit and tie are over.

Humor, my dear soldiers of sales, is your trusty sidekick in the charm offensive. A well-timed joke can do wonders. It's the sugar that makes the bitter pill of persuasion go down smoother. So, be the stand-up comedian of the sales floor, leaving your customers not just with a product but with a smile. Keep it professional and short and know when to stop. Trust me, I have a collection of dad jokes and funny Beavis and Butthead socks. Even if my jokes don't work, my socks will.

Act 2: The Product as a Hero

In our grand sales production, this is an easy one: the product isn't just a prop; it's the hero of our epic tale. But remember, every hero needs a compelling backstory. Know your product inside and out – its virtues, quirks, and how it can change lives (or at least make them a bit more adventurous). But keep it short. For every problem, there is a solution, and the solution is the product! *I love saying that phrase...*

TIP: When presenting the product as a hero, (AGAIN!) try a two second pause every now and then while you're presenting. This allows the listener to play this movie in their mind and keeps them engaged. Tell a story; don't make a prolonged statement.

Now, here comes the twist: Make your customer the co- hero of the story. Show them how this product is the missing piece to their life's puzzle, the sidekick they never knew they needed. It's not just a vacuum cleaner; it's the superhero of cleanliness, banishing dust bunnies and villains alike!

***TIP**: You might be selling something already in your portfolio, but when it comes time to create something new or find a new use for a current product, identify a problem first then create a solution. Ba-BAM! You just found your market. Now create how it can be inviting and used. Then SELL it!*

Act 3: Upselling Jedi Mind Trick

Ah, upselling – the Jedi mind trick of the sales universe. Mastering the art of convincing customers to go from "I'll take the basic package" to "Throw in the deluxe version!" requires finesse. It's not about pushing it; it's about suggesting. Plant the seed of desire, water it with perks and benefits, and watch it grow into a flourishing upsell.

***TIP**: Humor, once again, is your ally here. Crack a joke about how the deluxe version practically pays for itself (wink, wink), and suddenly, your customer is not just buying a product; they're investing in a lifestyle upgrade. Or! Be honest and say they do not need it. Sometimes honesty opens them up for more up-selling by earning trust. Again, selling yourself goes a lot farther.*

Look, we almost never NEED anything; we choose to have it. Let your customer know it's an offering, and it has benefits that are either savings, perks, or convenience. Beyond those things, your pitch may seem pushy or over the top. Know when, what, and how to offer additions.

***Financial TIP:** If you are buying something that you, or your client, will be financing, let them know it's not about the lump sum due right now, in reality it may be only adding $2 a month to the monthly payment. By breaking it down to $2 a month, it's no longer about a sticker shock of $6,000, it's about selling something for the price of a single candy bar a month. I say this all the time, "Why should I use my money when I can use the bank's."*

Act 4: Handling Objections Like a Pro

In this theatrical journey, objections are your plot twists. They add drama, suspense, and the opportunity for a brilliant comeback. When a customer raises an objection, don't panic – embrace it. It's your chance to shine, and even learn.

Use humor to diffuse tension. A witty remark can turn a potential roadblock into a mere speed bump on the customer's journey to purchase. But know when it's appropriate for humor. Remember, objections are not barriers; they're steppingstones to a successful sale. Be understanding from their perspective, relate, and tell your story. In the end, you cannot sell everyone, but leave on a positive note as if you want them to refer you to someone they know. If you do that, then you just sold yourself, and that's a sale.

It's OK to relate to your client and agree if they feel it's not for them. Be a good human and let them leave on a good note and like you, because whether you believe in Karma or not, things tend to randomly circle back.

TIP: Know when to step back or walk away! Your time has a value and if someone is 100% not going to be open to an alternative to their objections, move one. Some people will not be into you or the product, or both. Be respectful and kind and move on.

Act 5: The Grand Finale – Closing the Deal with Flair

As we approach the grand finale, it's time to close the deal with flair. The art of the close is a delicate dance. You've laid the groundwork with charm, made the product the hero, mastered the Jedi mind trick, and gracefully handled objections. Now, it's time for the bass drop like your favorite hype sound build up. Employ humor, excitement, and gratitude strategically in your closing statements. Create a sense of urgency with a playful quip or a limited time offer that's too good to pass up. Make your customers feel like they're not just buying a product; they're seizing an opportunity. FOMO (fear of missing out) is a real thing which is why you always hear about single day sales etc. But more so, make their experience enjoyable.

TIP: Seal the deal? Make them feel like they just won an award! Congratulate them and make them feel confident!

Story: *I'm a wristwatch guy and always wanted an Omega James Bond special edition watch, so when the stars aligned, the local Omega boutique reached out to me as they knew I was a big fan and this was a grail watch for me, and said, "We knew this is special for you and there's no better person we'd like to offer this to." This wasn't just any day either, this was beyond special. It was shipped into their location, but they went as far as to hold the watch for over a month until "International James Bond Day." I went out and rented a tux and on that day, I walked in, in full 007 form! I was greeted with a Martini (shaken not stirred of course) and made to feel appreciated, important, straight up Bond! They made this day unforgettable! I love sharing that moment. Then they, so smoothly, upsold my wife. Cause she HAD to have one now too ... Thank you for that ... Alex!*

The Encore: Building Long-Term Relationships

But wait, there's more! In the world of selling, every successful transaction is an invitation to a long-term relationship. Follow up with a personalized touch – a thank- you note, a joke in an email, or a discount for their next purchase. Follow up is a second first date! The experience you offered is almost more important than the product, you want to trigger those senses they originally got and want again like we discussed in Chapter 1.

The art of selling extends beyond the one-time deal; it's about creating a fan base. Your customers should not only be satisfied with their purchase but delighted by the entire experience. And, of course, they should be eager to recommend you to their friends, family, and the occasional stranger on the street.

Keep in mind, people are 1,000% more likely to socially share a bad experience versus a good one. Keep every experience as good as it can be, and if reviews drive your business, come up with a simple and easy way for them to leave a good one as early as possible.

TIP: A single sale is only good once. You want them to come back, and you want the referrals. Return business is a client base that spreads like wildfire ... and far surpasses a single sale. Same goes for relationships: it's a long game that you want to constantly offer your partner once committed. You can't relive the first 6 months, but you can create the next ones.

Customer Service IS Sales

Customer service is not just a follow-up and maintenance, it is a continuous reflection of you and your product. It needs to be a constant open door for sales. If a customer has a wonderful purchase, but later calls with an issue and doesn't get help, they will 100% not want to come back. Worse, they will also spread the negative word faster than chickenpox in a daycare. This will kill all of your marketing, branding, and sales efforts.

People are more trigger happy to post or share negative experiences than they are about a good one, unless asked. Again, a single sale is only that. Designing and providing a customer service plan should be a standard.

Here's some interesting sociology for you: People love drama. Some people *are* drama. Don't be on the wrong end of negative PR. The old saw about all PR being good PR no longer holds. Some bad PR is so bad you cannot come back from it – in the short term at least. With that said, more people are likely to complain about an experience rather than praise one, especially on social media. Which maybe is why we view social venting as a form of entertainment.

Let's use a car dealership for instance – *OMG I hope some dealership staff read this ....*

You sold a car, great job! Now you want the customer to tell all of their friends and post about it, right? So, you make that pickup day special, like Omega did for me. Then call that customer the next week and just ask if they are enjoying their new vehicle. Create a schedule for you to check in on them every few months, send holidays cards and birthday cards, and perhaps even help them when it's time for maintenance.

Your objective should be to create a lasting, positive experience that will influence how they feel about you and the dealership. You want them as long-term customers. Trade-ins are a thing, so are family members, new models, friends, etc. Whether you have a customer service department or are flying solo, your future with that customer depends on the after-sale experience.

Story: I had an Audi once and the local dealership hosted these great concerts, and charity and racing events which I looked forward to. These things tied me to this dealership and brand, not only as a consumer, but as a member of the group. It was fun and I loved the idea of belonging to a "car community." The events they held weren't only to pitch me to buy another vehicle; this was networking among like- minded people. I made new friends, we all enjoyed seeing each other, and we all essentially became brand ambassadors. That's worth far more than a commercial on public TV, by far.

Having this kind of communication with your customers goes a long way toward retention, networking, and reputation. No one should be too high up or busy to call a customer. My dealership's outreach offered a wholly positive experience. It is one I try to replicate in my businesses.

To wrap up this art of persuasion, here are some key takeaways.

1) Be knowledgeable and confident in what you are selling.

2) Be presentable and approachable with your first impression.

3) Speak well and tell a compelling story (try doing so with planned pauses).

4) Control your tone when speaking.

5) Use positive body language and gestures to gain engagement.

6) Be honest and transparent if there are objections. Respond to concerns with positive solutions.

7) Simply ask for the sale.

8) Be grateful, humble, and appreciative, deal or not.

9) Remember, you are a brand, and you want to leave any situation with a positive impression and lasting reputation. Not every deal gets sealed, but you never know who you will run into later in life, network with, or perhaps end up working for.

10) Last, hopefully you don't have to use it, but knowing when to walk away is just as powerful as closing the deal.

Chapter 8: The Soapbox

Do I mean you should actually stand on a soapbox? Well ... yes. Before the age of media and even before the age of the megaphone, standing on an old wooden shipping box and presenting your argument to a crowd was the way to draw attention and announce your product. Speeches often were made by merchants, salespeople, and even politicians from such a perch.

The concept was simple: through entertainment and storytelling, speakers would captivate and then sell their product, one by one, until the crowd rushed in. Sound familiar? Perhaps like a social media post or an ad that has 1+ million "Likes and Shares"? Oddly enough, when a video or a song or a product goes viral today, the situation is not unlike that of those people 200 years ago, who gathered around a charismatic soapbox speaker.

Today, we use the same concept. We just do so with new methods of delivery. We are now able to target the "crowd" through technology. But, instead of that crowd forming around a single person in a busy market who had a booming, boisterous voice, it's now a virtual crowd. But really, how many posts actually go viral? More importantly, how many posts convert to sales? Some products and people are just amazing, but they never get traction like, say, *"Bacon Flavored Jellyfish."* This is where understanding entertainment as a tool when selling comes in.

Our first soapbox of choice for advertising is now social media. Rightfully so. I don't need to go deep into it, but social media is available worldwide and is easily accessible through the use of the internet. This "digital soapbox" is basically free; it's so widely available that there's almost no way to avoid being exposed to it – unless you ditch the cell phone, all electronics, and live the backwoods life. But how do we captivate in such a realm with millions of others trying to do the same?

One way is through promotion, which is just another way of saying "you pay for it" to be broadcast, promoted, showcased, and even ranked. The other option? Well, it's a combination of creativity and techy stuff, such as algorithms. No matter which option you take, you're still trying to capture the attention of millions, and for most, you'd prefer to make money doing it.

It might sound odd in today's society but literally going out to a busy public place and, no joke, standing on a box and presenting to a crowd actually still works! Now, you don't see this public display often, as perhaps society is becoming introverted due to cell phones. When you do see this being done, it's usually indoors at tradeshows, expos, and special events. The funny thing is that event production companies and even industry leaders have now figured out that the old-fashioned soap box is so effective that it's become a lucrative business in itself! I mean, why not put on your own special tradeshow and automatically make yourself the branded name and own the spotlight?

The bottom line is that there are so many different types of soapboxes available; you just need to find out which offers the best audience, platform, and ROI for you.

Raw Presentation

When I say raw presentation, I'm not talking about winging a pitch out of nowhere. I'm talking about knowing your pitch and presentation and being able to do it in *the most lively form* possible. To do this, you've got to have a well-rehearsed script, the instincts and courage of an improv comedian, and the willingness to get in front of a live audience. It's new. It's raw. It's exciting.

Again, rehearse what it is you are presenting, practice your short script, and know each key point you want to hit. Be the comedian who knows the punchline, but still leads the audience through a story to get to it. Do the same. Know your punchline, practice ways to get to it that are engaging, and, when the time comes, you'll nail it. But remember, every crowd is different; watch for reactions and signals through body language and laughter. At the first hint of their losing interest, move on.

All of the very best salesmen I have ever known could nail a tagline, a joke, a reference in an instant. They also could present a well formulated pitch to an audience without ever giving off a salesman vibe. That's where you need to be!

Some of these best presenters do best in front of a crowd versus a meeting room, including myself. For me there is a sense of comfort with a large crowd, I know it sounds odd, but hear me out. For me, I can't see or catch the reactions of my listeners when there are so many. It's not like I'm engaging with all of them. Rather, it's like an actor on a stage: I get to act. I feel much less comfortable when I'm presenting to just a few people. I perform better in front of 20-10,000 people versus 10.

To each their own. However, if you feel nervous in a crowd or are an introvert, here's a little trick: Look out past the first rows of people, to a person in the back – even an imaginary person, in the back. You see, there is a sense of ease that comes with speaking to someone 50ft away vs 5ft. If you have ever felt nervous in front of a crowd, practice this. Feel the distance between you and that person in the back of the crowd.

The anxiety you're feeling comes from the perspective of a close-in personal space, which increases your ability to recognize reactions, whether they are physical cues or verbal cues. The more confined the space, the more you are hunting for reactions. By speaking to your imaginary friend at the back of the room, you won't be waiting for reactions or cringing when they're not what you want. You'll simply be telling a story to a friend. Move around the stage with your eyes scanning the room. Don't stop moving; it will help you relax. Be sure to use your best body language.

TIP: *It's going to be tough for some, but find a way to relax, even fool yourself, before entering the space. If you're speaking in front of 1-10 people, fuzz them out like the Matrix and run through your rehearsed key points. If you're speaking in front of a crowd, look to the back and speak to those you want to draw in versus those who are already in front of you. Once you do this, your voice will carry, you will feel at ease, and you will perform like you do in the shower.*

Trade Shows

Okay, most professionals have attended a trade show or expo in some form. What you see when you enter the convention center are rows and rows of businesses that feature their exhibits. Up and down the aisles, you will see businessmen walking, talking, and congregating. All of them – whether a corporation or a single businessman – are on their own "soapbox," whether in their 10x10 square foot space or on the floor, putting themselves forth to capture attention, market their brand, gain clients, and even take orders on the fly. The questions each and every one of them is asking themself, over and over again as people stream past their booth, are *Will they stop? How do I stop them? How do I pitch the product? How do I get their attention?*

If you find yourself in this situation or even pitching in a random location, there are a few tricks I've used in the past to promote and stand out, which I will share with you. Keep in mind that not all products are showstoppers or have the WOW factor; some are less than sexy, and, honestly, some have no use in life at all.

Here's a little tip if you are looking to stand out in a crowd or a tradeshow arena, no matter the product:

1) First, you may not be the only one there promoting that product or service. Do your research and find out who the others are. Know your approach *and theirs*, so you can present differently. Be sneaky: learn where you stand against the others. Sometimes standing out is as simple as letting

your own more appealing personality shine. Be approachable and fun. Turn on the charm. But don't be pitchy. You just have to out market the others.

2) Ditch the swag and giveaways. Most are cheap products that leave no impression on potential clients and no ROI. Stop with the pens, coin holders, koozies, and bottle openers. Those cheap items are not going to get anyone to remember you as quality or the go-to salesperson. Be creative: if you plan to use a giveaway to draw people to your booth, use quality swag, such as food, lotto tickets, heck even kids' toys! Toys?! Yes sir! Most professionals have families and coming home with something for their kid might make a more lasting impression than a mouse pad. After all, you live with your kiddos and not with a mouse pad. Just think outside the box. If your thing is to give away items with your brand on it, are you cheap or quality? What you give away reflects that choice.

3) If marketing inside the trade show is too costly, do it outside the show! Super easy trick here: find out through the city if you can block the street or parking meters and do a massive showing at a fraction of the cost. Check into this well before the event. Use this space for displays, exhibits, showcasing the company vehicle, or even entertainment. Why rent a booth when you can own the street? You can also host an event right after the trade show ends. Not kidding here. I've spent a fraction of the cost and got more buyers to attend my solo branded event than it would have cost for a 10x10ft booth inside.

4) Inside and want to stand out? Fun one here ... buy a custom logo laser projector, put it at your booth and project on the ceiling or large wall inside the show. Not all allow this, but even if they don't, it will take some time until you get asked to move! But don't be too quick to pack it up! I've used the same logo projector at nighttime to project on downtown buildings, in bars, and even on sidewalks! These are just simple things to help you stand out over the other 100 booths just like yours.

5) Socialize and network. Sounds simple, but simply standing at a booth might come across like a circling shark ready to pounce, which might make people avoid your space. Hell, I have. Be fun and welcoming. Network before the event, set up meet up times at your space, walk around and promote, don't be static. And look, if someone has to ask what it is that you and your team do, you are failing already. Work on a great display and simple message.

6) Last one of many. This is not for the faint of heart but bring your soapbox. Literally. Sounds crazy I know, but it works because you instantly command attention! Stand up for all to see and *pitch with humor*. As folks gather around you like seagulls around a bag of chips, others will notice the unexpected interruption, see the growing crowd, and their natural instincts will draw them over to see what the bustle is. And if you are not the public pitchman type, hire one for the day. Your actions will be more widely remembered than a give-a-way key chain. Any time I got more than

5 people in front of the booth, people ALWAYS started to gather to see what the deal was.

A warning: If you think that you're going to set up a booth at a huge trade show and magically seal dozens of deals, jokes on you. That's almost never the case – unless you have put together a pre-show plan of attack. Oh, you might meet a new client and do some networking, but if you want the tradeshow to bring in clients, help you make deals, and introduce you to new contacts, you need a plan. You need to be thinking about making each day that you are clocked in your personal trade show.

How do I stand out? What is my opening pitch? How do I get the crowd to gather around my space? A driven mindset will help you understand not just that your days will be challenging, but that every day should be better than the last. You need to hone in on what works, and organize your time and resources for the highest level of productivity.

Although trade shows are designed to fill the floor with tons of potential buyers who are there to see the latest and greatest, unless you really get to work, you are also potentially missing other opportunities that are right in front of you. What I mean by this is that the show could be filled with networking gold. Be open minded. See the other exhibitors, staff, and even competitors as potential clients. Even if they do not buy in, they may know someone who will.

This brings us to a sneaky approach to expanding your reach through the network of others.

Finding Your Soapbox

There are many different approaches to marketing and sales. Some methods are personal, some are natural habits or comfort zones, and a lot of others are results driven. What I suggest is that you look at *every situation* as an opportunity to present. Think of it as being on your own soapbox, whether it's online or in person. The more you practice 'being on your soapbox' (your pitch and presentation), the more comfortable you will become at it, and the more comfortable you are, the better presenter you will be. Be sure to read the room and know your target audience first, plan your timing to be the most fitting, and hop on the box.

Not everyone is a natural public speaker, but everyone is a presenter when they are engaged with like-minded others and feel comfortable in their own domain. If you want to be that trade show speaker, be the face of a brand, or a public speaker, there are some key points that I have learned that work every time.

Here are a few pointers.

• Prepare for the meet, event, or date. Know your objective and end goal.

• Rehearse some of the more simple quips you have, your key points, and your responses to some of the most common questions. Write them down, type them up, or give the speech to your mirror ... out loud. By doing so, you will be prepared.

• Knowing your responses to questions is key, but how do you psychically react? Are you smooth? Nervous? Do you fumble? The more you practice your responses, the more natural you will be in person.

• Lastly, engage. You *will* get responses. Knowing how to react and reengage and carry the conversation is how you will create a bond with your listener.

TIP: Every industry, every job, and every relationship use some form of initial approach to pitch. Reflect back on the times you stood on your soapbox. What were the results? Try to learn from each effort. Explore how you could have done better. Listen and respond to those who have questions. In doing so, you will form a bond through your own responses. Such interactions create trust – that's how you close a sale.

Chapter 9: Backdoor Sales

For most people who have worked in marketing and sales, you have been told to knock on doors, to go after your top and biggest clients directly, and to always try to get at least a foot in the door. I'm going to tell you that if the front door proves tough, try the back door. I'm not talking about stalking them on their fire escapes: I'm talking about finding creative ways to get your target client's attention.

This is perhaps a common scenario: say you have a big corporate client that you've been trying to get in front of forever, but you cannot get a call back, no one will meet with you, and you have been strong-armed in as if you were walking into the Fort Knox lobby and met by a receptionist with a black belt. You've exhausted all your efforts. How, you wonder, did the others get in? Well, first of all, you've *not* exhausted all of your efforts. It's not time to give up; it's time to be creative! Ditch the gifts, the email blasts, the cold calls, and the door knocking ... just find a way in the back-door. No matter what industry you are in or selling, there are hidden doorways to every situation and everyone.

"Okay, buddy," you say. "Where is this backdoor?"

What I consider a backdoor is an indirect and subtle approach to gaining access to or marketing to new clients. Instead of the cold calling, in-your-face direct methods, you have to be creative and find the little ways to catch their attention or pique their interest right off the bat. Or play the long game, which is to create brand awareness. Yes, putting a face to a name, shaking a hand, or even making someone laugh in person has more weight than most approaches, and there is a time and a place for those things, but what we are talking about is how do you get to that interaction, if all you are getting are roadblocks and a special forces-trained doorman?

First, identify how your client may be able to use your service or product. This should be the number one catch for a salesperson: create a use. I know this sounds simple, and we get it: you can sell anything and all you want is a chance at their business. But clients don't always buy off value; they often buy off emotion. After all, buying something is a choice. So, once you find out why they NEED your product or have use for it, get creative. Start off by finding out what other services or products, that are not your direct competitors, are already used by your client. Let's say you want to sell that company something as simple and as non- sexy as toilet paper.

Well, find out who their plumbers are. Find out who is in their maintenance department. Explore the names of their suppliers and distributors for literally anything. Then approach those people directly. Try to gain at least one *as a client* – more if you can. Keep working on them.

Eventually, enough of that company's vendors will be using you that the big client will begin to recognize your brand or name.

By developing collaborations with people already in the door, you've just walked your company through the back door, all while making money doing so. This is my backdoor approach. It's a crafty way to brand and market yourself or your company directly, but also indirectly. Going through the back door may take a little more time and effort, but by branding yourself as the go-to, you'll start to network in through those already in. Again, this works with any product or service; you start by finding out who works within the company and their vendors. Trust me, their vendors already have the contact you want; it's your job to figure out how to get them to share it.

I've personally used this tactic and it's worked every time. I'll even go as far as connecting on professional networking sites with staff from my target client just to break the ice and leave little cues prior to pitching to them. By the time I have directly reached out to the potential customer, they had either already heard of me, or they had heard of our business, which brings down their guard and allows for a lower tension environment. That is when you can casually approach them. But don't pitch them right away; give them some breathing room, otherwise they will run, block, and delete as fast as your weekend's browser history. Then, all of your efforts will have been wasted.

There are many ways to get in the front, back, or even the side door. Consider the Trojan Horse approach. Send breakfast once a week to their office? Sponsor a charity event with them? Cross promote them online? What about hosting an event and inviting all clients casually? Don't expect an ROI within days; branding trust is earned over time.

TIP: Everyone needs to eat and likes food but should your gifts of food not do the trick, be different. Be creative. Order them a $50 golf putting green for the breakroom, stock their fridge with fun snacks and treats, give everyone a tiny desk plant. Donuts and fatty foods will just carb people out and be thrown away that day.

Casual approaches work because people like to have fun, be treated well, and enjoy the perks of the job, more so at the bottom. The exec's get it all, but the influencers might be at a lower position. Drop your guard, be an honest and good person, be transparent, and those people will create a good opinion about you and your business. Sometimes, that is all you need. By taking this approach, you are networking to get a foot in the door. And, on that note, let's touch on a new approach: it's selling without selling; most people call it networking.

Networking

Networking, in general, is a monumental tool for any business or profession. You should always have the mindset of "collect them all" – as you never know who you will come across later or how you might be able to leverage the relationship. As you meet others inside and outside of the professional environment, always be mindful that not everyone is in your line of work or has the same background or skill set as you. But as you grow your network, you will ultimately find that there will come a situation where you need an industry insider or an expert or even help gaining new clients. That is where the relationships in your network just might come in handy.

A network is considered a portfolio of individuals you have interacted with, that can be in the same industry you are, or industries outside your profession, through which you can leverage to gain knowledge and/or assess resources. Not too long ago, networking was limited to those whose business card you had or whose phone number was in your rolodex. With today's technology and platforms, you can literally network around the world in seconds. You need to be networking daily. Literally, no one is going to do this for you, so spend 10 minutes a day and network through whatever online platform you choose.

TIP: Send at least 10 minutes a day on a professional networking platform and try to make new connections within your target clients, but also reach out to anyone and EVERYONE. Expand your own brand as much as you can.

It's inevitable, you will gain some traction with someone at some point. When this happens, you've grown your brand and that can translate to SALES!

Okay! Once you have established a growing network, no matter whom you've met or what industry they're in, it's a great practice to professionally send a follow-up. A simple way to do this is to shoot out a simple "thank you" or "great to meet you" email, or even a quick phone call. By doing so, you've opened up the networking opportunity, given out all of your professional contact information, and left an impression on those people. Remember, you are selling yourself and your personal brand first. Take the time to leave these little impressions. Like I said, you never know; they might share your info with someone else.

__TIP:__ I tend to give it a couple of days before reaching out to a new connection. Depending on when and where I met them, this allows some decompression time. Crowding or being pushy never works. Take it easy, be methodic, welcoming, and low pressure. I don't go in for the kill on my first connection with a new contact. I keep my initial follow-up simple, short, grateful, and open ended.

A lot of what I have touched on isn't all that complicated; there are millions of people who use and discuss these topics on a daily basis. You'll soon be able to recognize the little things that make big impacts, and even start to leverage this knowledge to your benefit. There are a few final things I want to touch base on. One of those things is the science behind why we are captivated, intrigued, and interested in what is being sold to us.

Making a sale comes down to an emotional reaction, so let's learn why. There is a science to how we all perceive, relate, and react. But what if I were to tell you that you *can* know how to control and influence reactions? Would you think this is a money-making superpower? If you said yes, you're not far off. And yes, there is a science to it.

Chapter 10: It's Science

(aka the Techy Stuff – once you get it, use it.)

Ha! You made it! Now, are you ready for the heavy brain science? If you're like me at this point, the answer is *HELL NO!* Don't worry, it's not as complicated as it sounds and it's absolutely fascinating. I've included this chapter because at the core of selling is psychology. What goes on in our heads is crazy. But understanding it will give you a leg up on the competition and will also make life make a little more sense.

It turns out that there *is* a science to us all and it starts with a little brain chemistry. Knowing what some of the chemicals are and how they influence memory and mood are the underlying secrets to opinions, influence, and decision making. Understanding some of the basics will help you understand the whys and the WTFs.

There were some big words I was going to add in here that breaks down the real science, but my editor literally told me I sounded like a medical textbook, so I'll put it into more simple terms and add some fun (sounds-like) humor, so I don't lose you at the end of the entire book. You're welcome.

So, let's kick off with taste – the rockstar of our sensory experiences. Imagine biting into your favorite pizza or savoring a plate of gooey chocolate cake. It's not just a treat for your taste buds; it's a chemical concert. With a bit of chocolate, our brains flush with key chemicals that take center stage. Releasing or storing serotonin *(sarah-toe-nin)* and dopamine *(dope-a-mean)*, the brain can change a mood, elevate the spirits, and ward off anxiety. Serotonin stabilizes moods and ensures the sensory party doesn't go off the rails, like that one time you partied with non-related Uncle Rico in Jamaica. Dopamine is the pleasure seeker that spreads joy wherever it goes. And then there's Adrenaline *(a-dren-a-lynn)*, the thrill-seeker that kicks in when excitement peaks, adding an extra kick to the festivities, good or bad.

Now, onto touch – the unsung hero. Whether it's the silky touch of that fuzzy purple couch at that nightclub you once went to or a warm hug from a friend, touch is more than physical; it's an emotional rollercoaster. Take *oxytocin (oxy- toe-sin)*, the "cuddle hormone," that transforms every touch into a heartwarming memory, fosters bonds and etches moments into our neural archives.

***TIP:** Occasionally we're offered wine, beer or champagne while we're out shopping or attending a corporate meeting. They're not trying to get the party started: they are trying to break down your personal walls and influence some of our brain chemistry in order to make you spend money or make you relax a little. Nothing wrong with either of those things. Take that drink and hang out a little. Enjoy the moment and live a little, courtesy of your slightly altered brain chemistry.*

As we navigate this carnival of sensations, products and experiences all fight for the spotlight in the grand theater of our minds. They aim to be the unforgettable act, the one you can't stop thinking about. So, what happens to your brain when you relish a meal, smell something familiar, or step on, I swear, the largest and sharpest Lego ever created? It's like getting a front-row ticket to the greatest show on Earth – the carnival within your mind.

Stay with me here ....

In order to unravel the intricate dance between sensory stimuli and the brain's inner workings, we'll explore some of the reasons behind our mental curtains and uncover a few details of how these chemical influencers create our memories.

(Take a break here if you need to, science is not eve-ryone's strong suit, I get it. But if everything in life is trying to sell you and fight for one of those rare memory brain cells, trying to understand how it works makes a lot of sense. It does all come together!)

Now, imagine biting into a crisp, warm Chimichanga (for those not in the south, that's a fried burrito). The crunch sends auditory signals, activating sound perception regions. Simultaneously, your taste buds decode sweet and whole-some notes, and then release dopamine for an overall pleas-urable experience. As you might imagine, the elements of food alone (the crunch, the taste) can trigger more of our in-ternal sensors than almost anything else! Food encompasses many of the components of a memory: smell, taste, texture ... just about everything that makes a memory. That is why having a meal is considered to be one of the most memora-ble of all experiences. Mmmm!!! FOOD!!!!

Beyond food, what about physically charged experi-ences? Like when the kids are gone and it's date night? Ahhh. Yup, you know where this is going – even if kids are not your thing yet, something as simple as another's physi-cal touch can (will) take center stage in your brain. Yes. I'm talking about sex here. Touch creates sensual excitement which causes the releases of endorphins (*in- door-fins*) and oxytocin (*oxy-toe-sin*) which, in turn, fosters feelings of ex-citement, happiness, and warmth. You know the feelings! As we all know, sex sells in many forms. I hope the reason *why it sells* makes more sense now. Sex is so powerful because of the pleasure chemicals that are released during the big show.

TIP: Hey, don't overthink this science stuff. Embrace it! You may never use the word oxytocin (oxy-toe-sin) again but trying to understand what is going on inside our brains is worth the mental exertion. Understanding how we work can be tremendously empowering.

There has got to be hundreds of words and terms for all that is going on inside our brains, and I promised my editor to not go off the deep end, but there are a couple terms that helped me understand a little more. By understanding these three chemicals, perhaps you can stimulate them to influence a situation or even someone. So, take a deep breath, and sound them out if you have to ...

Serotonin (sarah-toe-nin): In the world of neurochemistry, this mood-stabilizing ringmaster influences our emotional landscape. Serotonin is like the "happy chemical" as it relates to all things that influence happiness. Serotonin acts like a backdrop and mood setter. Consider mood or sleep: serotonin affects both of these, and more. Think of serotonin as a key to the door of our moods. If you want to influence the mood of the room and the mood of the buyer to be more relaxed, you might soften the lighting or light a candle or simply to try to manage yourself in a more Zen way. Calmness begets calmness.

Dopamine (*dope-a-mean*), Dopamine, our pleasure dealer, reinforces behaviors linked to reward. Now serotonin and dopamine are both associated with happiness, but dopamine gives you that drive or desire to chase it and the reward from it. Imagine longing for your favorite dish or a comforting touch, like that of date night. It is possible that you chase dopamine, this feel-good hormone, in your daily life. In marketing and sales, you want to trigger in your client a desire to chase a memory, a desire, or a feeling. Because that can lead to closing the sale – which is when they will get the satisfaction they are searching for. This can be done not just for big ticket sales, but even for customer service. Try mirroring their energy or excitement; reference why they are working with you; when speaking, try to elevate them more with your words of appreciation; and compliment them and the item. Your customer is working with you for a reason, make them feel good about it, no matter the product.

Adrenaline (*a-dren-a-lynn*), And then there is the addictive, the electrifying force that transforms ordinary moments into unforgettable memories. Released in response to stress or excitement, adrenaline adds a thrilling dimension. Think of the excitement or nervousness of getting pulled over by a cop or the heart-pounding thrill of a first date. ... Or, for some, that time you got fired. This is also where those stomach 'Butterflies' come from. Adrenaline can be released in good, bad, and even terrifying situations. This monumental natural injection can give what some people feel is a high, hence the term "Adrenaline Junky."

There are different levels of adrenaline. And different people are stimulated in different ways. For some, finally getting your dream date might stimulate huge adrenaline. For others, it might be the sound of a powerful sports car. There are a couple of different ways to spark this adrenaline in your customers. One might be the excitement and energy offered during the sale process. Again, excitement can be catching! Another way is to surround them with what they are looking for. If your gig is selling powerful sports cars to enthusiasts, make sure you put them in the driver's seat and hand them the keys – even starting the engine will flood them with adrenaline. Be excited for your customer and help influence that ending result.

TIP: Our sensory experiences aren't isolated events; they're the shoelaces of memory. Remember the feeling of that first date? Skydiving? Favorite restaurant? These memories are directly tied to a sensation you experienced. Simply put, sensations create memories.

Now, let's unveil the mystery of memory a little. How do our brains turn fleeting sensations into enduring memories that influence our preferences and decisions? This is what you want to be a master at when selling a product or personal impression! If you can create a memory, you'll have a foot in the door.

Look at our sensory experiences, which bombard us from all angles – visual, auditory, smell, taste, and touch, shape almost everything a memory is created by. As we engage with our surroundings, this information reaches brain regions for processing where it subconsciously decides to keep or ditch it as a memory.

So, picture strolling through a bustling marketplace. The colors, the sounds, and even the scent of street tacos and cotton candy converge deep in our brain, forming a multi-sensory memory or perhaps bringing back a past one. But how do memories get prioritized to be either stored or ditched? This is where understanding the science will help you create a lasting impression. You want to learn to *influence* memories. (Yep, be an influencer.) In reality, we all do this on a daily basis without thinking. From how we dress, to cleaning our house before guests, to adding Zen incense to the office space, and so on, we are creating memories. We are trying to create an impression and a positive memory, no matter the size.

Memories: Every person has not only their own opinion; they also have different interests and dislikes. Think about the great dinner party you threw last month. Each person at that party might equally feel that it was a great night. But each of their memories of that evening will be different.

Each will remember something that spoke specifically to them, which they found special: the wine, the flowers, the conversation, the flirtation with the new guy.

Knowing that you can influence an environment in all these different ways will make a dramatic difference in how you create a memorable dinner party. It is no different in sales and marketing. Both share the same goal: to have a great night (or a great meeting). So, use what you already have stored upstairs to create a memorable event. Try to create a memory for your client.

Have you ever seen a billboard that only features a loaf of bread, or one that shows a toasted sandwich, oozing with melted cheese, and the image stays fresh in your mind? That is because the aroma of freshly baked bread has become linked in your mind with the visual of that billboard, creating a robust memory. Do you like cotton candy? What if you saw a picture of fluffy pink cotton candy? For many, that image of cotton candy swiftly brings up your memory of your dad buying you a wand of cotton candy at the local festival or fair. All it took was the visual to trigger an associated memory. In digital and print marketing, where you cannot touch, smell, hear or taste, they sell you on via visuals. In marketing you are trying to trigger a sensory memory, and in sales, you are trying to create one in real time.

***TIP**: From a bakery to candles, to that freaking store in the mall that sprays their branded cologne all over the clothes (gag). They are playing to your sensors of memories. Try the same around yourself as well. It's so simple to add a hidden detail to your home, workplace, and yourself, for that matter, that just might play a sneaky role in how others experience the meeting or the event. This could be as easy as wearing a fun bow tie to the fresh scent of your office.*

~

We've now gone through some simple science about how to create a memorable situation by invoking an emotional reaction. Emotions play a pivotal role in our lives, as they are integral to our memories. Emotionally charged experiences imprint into our memories with startling clarity, standing out from more neutral events. An example might be winning a lottery ticket. That would be a powerful memory. An interaction with a rude person might be equally powerful. Though negative and unwanted, it is still a memory.

Your brain stores your memories based on the power of your emotional reaction, both good and bad. To illustrate: Do you remember every time you lost on a scratch off lottery ticket? No? Huh ... that's weird. Must just be me. What about remembering the one time you hit it big? Do you remember that one? This dance between emotions and memory weaves each experience throughout every day of our lives. Sometimes without our even knowing.

What we experience, such as noises, smells, touch, and emotions all create a memory. Some memories are more memorable than others. Some people have amazing capacities to remember everything, but for the rest of us, it takes an experience to own that brain cell. As a salesperson, it is to your great benefit to create an experience that your client will remember, because making that happen – making your client remember you and your product – is one of the most important things any marketing or sales professional can do.

As we conclude this chapter on big word science-y words, try to ponder the profound implications of understanding how our minds are stimulated. Sensory experiences aren't fleeting; they are threads in the intricate fibers of our memories. By unraveling the neuro-scientific big words, we can gain a deeper appreciation for the richness of our cognitive landscape.

Okay. Enough science.

Now that you've gotten a crash course of brain stimulants and how they work, it's time to start implementing these into your life as a top salesperson. Remember, everything you say and do can influence your surroundings, as well as your emotions and those of those around you. Leverage the senses to your advantage by understanding what each can do and make your experiences memorable.

Curtain Call

As the curtain falls on our whimsical exploration of the art of marketing and selling, remember that every salesperson is an artistic performer. Your stage is the sales floor, your palette is humor and charm, and your masterpiece is a satisfied audience buying into not just your product, but you.

Whether you are in marketing, sales, or even on a date, the first thing is always remember, you are a product and there is not another like you. You hold what makes you unique and creative; whether you know it or not, you already have been given all the keys to success. Success for some is the feeling of a win, for others it's material tangibles, and for still others, it's a happy family. Success is gained by achieving goals, some of which are set by others, some of which are personal. Challenge yourself but make some goals attainable like a well-planned benchmark.

In the grand masterpiece of salesmanship, your legacy is not just the products you sold but the smiles you created, the dreams you fulfilled, and the laughter that echoed through the hallowed halls of the sales arena. So, go forth with humor in your heart, charm in your step, and the unwavering belief that, indeed, everything is for sale, everything is selling you – you just need to know how to sell it back.

Keep in mind, you are also selling your personal brand first. Even if you didn't make the sale, always keep your brand at the highest level. Even if you change jobs or relationships, your brand has a value and reputation.

The stage is yours and take advantage of this deal before it's too late!

ACT NOW!

(DJ gets on the mic with that deep DJ voice ...)

"Alllll right ... next up on stage is Charisma from New Orleans!"

To all of my readers – you're welcome for that ongoing bad joke.

Motivational, Yet True.

~You cannot change the past, but you can influence the future.

~ If you hate your job, try to be the best at it; it will piss off more people, and then everyone wins.

~ If you feel lost, go look in the mirror and if you can smile, you just found yourself. Start there.

~ Is the glass half full or half empty? Either way, there's a glass that resembles opportunity. What you put in or take away from it is up to you.

~ If you are trying to find a work / life balance. Stop. There will never be a balance, as we all are meant to live life, not live work.

~ Most people don't take risks due to fear of failure. If you don't try, you've failed anyway.

~ If someone uses fear as a tactic, they're losing to their own insecurity.

~ A thank you without words can mean more than saying it for years.

You've reached the last page.

Author Bio

Jay Kriner is an accomplished serial entrepreneur, viral product creator, and executive known for his innovative approach across multiple industries. His journey to prominence began in 2012 as he finally broke out with his patented beverage holding belt buckle, which gained nationwide recognition on the TV show *Shark Tank*, radio and publications. He has paved his own way through many diverse entrepreneurial ventures, including roles as a U.S. government contractor, festival producer, co-bar owner, and founder of a design and consulting firm. Jay's knack for identifying market opportunities and his fearless entrepreneurial spirit have also helped launch successful businesses for others, solidifying his reputation as a multi- industry innovator and influencer.

In 2024, Jay distilled his extensive experience and insights into his first book, *"Butterflies - The Performance and Psychology of Sales."* The book offers a fresh perspective on sales, focusing on the psychological aspects and emotional challenges that define success in the field. Drawing from his personal journey and professional achievements, Jay aims to inspire readers to leverage their fears and anxieties as catalysts for growth and success.

Jay's narrative is more than a collection of success stories; it's a blueprint for embracing innovation, understanding the human element in business, and achieving excellence. His diverse career and contributions to various fields demonstrate his versatile talent and unwavering commitment to making a significant impact.

As creative as Jay is, this book was released tandem alongside another book title, *"Bacon Flavored Jellyfish,"* which includes the same content, but in his true form, was a social experiment to see if one would gain more interest than the other solely based off the cover art which had nothing more to do with than eye catching "clickbait."

TopSalesBook.com

From Me to You,

First, thank you for buying this book and spending some time with it. I tried to put as much knowledge, creativity, and fun onto the pages as I could.

To be honest, I'm not much of a reader and I've always hated writing emails, let alone essays. This project took me 10 years to start, 9 months to write, and 1 awesome editor (Katie Hall) to tell me to rewrite it at least 24 times. In the end, I found myself caught nightly going through and adding, deleting, and trying to put something on paper that relates to real life. I've tried to craft material for my readers that is actually usable and hopefully it changes some lives.

In the end, LIVE life more.

Enjoy everything around you; if you do, people will naturally gravitate towards you, and never forget, pushy people suck. Don't be pushy. Be a buyer first and buyers will buy in, because there's nothing worse than someone who doesn't drink their own Kool-Aid.

~ Jay K.

~ Very special thanks to my beautiful wife for putting up with me! Go Dodgers! ~